PATTERNS OF POETRY

PATTERNS OF POETRY

An Encyclopedia of Forms

MILLER WILLIAMS

LOUISIANA STATE UNIVERSITY PRESS

BATON ROUGE

Copyright © 1986 by Louisiana State University Press
Manufactured in the United States of America

Designer: Albert Crochet
Typeface: Linotron Palatino
Typesetter: G&S Typesetters, Inc.

Library of Congress Cataloging in Publication Data

Williams, Miller.
  Patterns of poetry.

  Bibliography: p.
  Includes index.
  1. Versification.   2. English poetry.   I. Title.
PN1042.W514   1986   808.1   85-23719
ISBN 0-8071-1253-4
ISBN 0-8071-1330-1 (pbk.)

Louisiana Paperback Edition, 1987
08 07   06   05   04   03
12   11   10

The paper in this book meets the guidelines for
permanence and durability of the Committee on
Production Guidelines for Book Longevity of the
Council on Library Resources.(∞)

Contents

Acknowledgments

T. Alan Broughton, John Ciardi, John Cowell, Martha Estes, Elisabeth Grant-Gibson, Larry Guinn, John Clellon Holmes, Ben Kimpel, Bill Nugent, Jeanie Pittman, Jean Rogers, Robert Ross, Stephanie Stearns, Cyrus and Martha Sutherland, James Whitehead, and, as always, Jordan Williams helped this book on its way. I am enduringly grateful.

A special thanks to Lewis Turco, whose respect for the forms of poetry has done much to keep them in our minds over the past decades. This book takes an approach different from his in the fine *Book of Forms*, but both grew out of the same fascination with the patterns that has fired our conversations for twenty-five years.

"Bread" by Jonathan Aldrich is reprinted from *Croquet Lover at the Dinner Table* by Jonathan Aldrich, by permission of the University of Missouri Press and the author. Copyright 1977 by Jonathan Aldrich.

"Granny Dean" is reprinted by permission of the author from *Against the Blues*, published by Broadside Press. Copyright 1972 by Alvin Aubert.

Lines from "Judith," translated by Ann Babb, reprinted by permission of the translator. Copyright 1980 by Ann Babb.

"My Grandfather's Church Goes Up" by Fred Chappell is reprinted by permission of Louisiana State University Press and the author from *Midquest* by Fred Chappell. Copyright 1981 by Fred Chappell.

"It took me some time to agree . . ." by John Ciardi is reprinted from *Limericks: Too Gross*, by Isaac Asimov and John Ciardi, by permission of W. W. Norton & Company, Inc. Copyright 1978 by W. W. Norton & Company, Inc.

"Men marry what they need . . ." by John Ciardi is reprinted by permission of the author from *I Marry You* by John Ciardi, published by Rutgers University Press. Copyright 1958 by John Ciardi.

"Talking Myself to Sleep at One More Hilton" by John Ciardi is reprinted by permission of the author from *This Strangest Everything* by

John Ciardi, published by Rutgers University Press. Copyright by John Ciardi.

Lines from "To Lucasta, About That War" by John Ciardi are reprinted by permission of the author from *39 Poems*, by John Ciardi, published by Rutgers University Press. Copyright 1959 by John Ciardi.

"Tenzone" by John Ciardi is reprinted by permission of the author from *Person to Person* by John Ciardi, published by Rutgers University Press. Copyright 1964 by John Ciardi.

"Encounter" and "Washing Your Feet" by John Ciardi are reprinted by permission of the author from *The Little That Is All* by John Ciardi, published by Rutgers University Press. Copyright 1974 by John Ciardi.

"An Apology for a Lost Classicism" by John Ciardi is reprinted by permission of the author. Copyright 1985 by John Ciardi.

"Gold Watch at Sixty" by William Cole is reprinted by permission of the author.

The poems of Wesli Court are reprinted by permission of the author.

The Welsh poems translated by Wesli Court are reprinted by permission of the translator from *The Airs of Wales*, a chapbook special issue of the Temple University *Poetry Newsletter*. Copyright 1981 by Wesli Court.

"For My Contemporaries" and "Friend, on this scaffold . . ." by J. V. Cunningham are from *The Collected Poems and Epigrams* by J. V. Cunningham, 1971, Swallow Press. Reprinted with the permission of Ohio University Press, Athens.

"Shelley," copyright 1936, 1964 by Robert Francis, is reprinted from *Robert Francis: Collected Poems, 1936–1976* (University of Massachusetts Press, 1976).

"Tiresias" by George Garrett is reprinted by permission of the author and the University of Arkansas Press from *Collected Poems of George Garrett*. Copyright 1984 by George Garrett.

Lines from "The Narcissiad" by R. S. Gwynn are reprinted by permission of the publisher from *The Narcissiad*. Copyright by Cedar Rock Press.

"Higgledy-Piggledy Euclid Geometer . . ." and "Higgledy-Piggledy Thomas A. Edison . . ." by Anthony Harrington are reprinted by permission of Hendricks Publishing Co. from *Tersery Versery* by Anthony Harrington. Copyright 1982 by Anthony Harrington.

"Word from Under" and "The Whereabouts" by Michael Heffernan are reprinted by permission of the publisher from *The Cry of Oliver Hardy* by Michael Heffernan. Copyright 1979, The University of Georgia Press.

"A Colloquy of Silences" and "Acrostic on a Line from Tom T. Hall" by Michael Heffernan are reprinted by permission of the author. Copyright 1984 by Michael Heffernan.

"Nightsong: Ferris Wheel by the Sea" by Edward Hirsch is reprinted by permission of Alfred A. Knopf from *For the Sleepwalkers*, copyright 1981 by Edward Hirsch.

"Traditional Red" by Robert Huff is reprinted by permission of the author from *The Ventriloquist: New and Selected Poems* by Robert Huff, University of Virginia Press. Copyright 1977 by Robert Huff.

"The Rural Carrier Stops to Kill a Nine-Foot Cottonmouth" by T. R. Hummer is reprinted by permission of Louisiana State University Press from *The Angelic Orders* by T. R. Hummer, copyright 1982 by T. R. Hummer.

"The Cannon Ball" and "We Filed Our Teeth on Trouble" by Dan Jaffe are reprinted from *Dan Freeman* by Dan Jaffe by permission of University of Nebraska Press. Copyright © 1967 by the University of Nebraska Press.

"Lady in Waiting" by Dan Jaffe is reprinted by permission of the author. Copyright 1984 by Dan Jaffe.

The poems of Donald Justice are reprinted by the permission of the author.

"A Dream near Water" by Sidney Lea is reprinted by permission of the University of Illinois Press from *Searching the Drowned Man*, by Sidney Lea, copyright 1980 by Sidney Lea.

"Not Marble nor the Gilded Monuments" by Archibald MacLeish is from *New and Collected Poems 1917–1976* by Archibald MacLeish. Copyright 1976 by Archibald MacLeish. Reprinted by permission of Houghton Mifflin Company.

"The Outing" by Dan Masterson is reprinted by permission of the University of Illinois Press from *On Earth as It Is* by Dan Masterson, copyright 1978 by Dan Masterson.

"The Black and Small Birds of Remorse" by Jo McDougall is reprinted by permission of the author from *Women Who Marry Houses*, published by Coyote Love Press. Copyright 1983 by Jo McDougall.

"About Opera" and "The Illiterate" by William Meredith are reprinted by permission of Alfred A. Knopf from *Earthwalk: New and*

"For the Life of Him and Her" by Reed Whittemore from *The Mother's Breast and the Father's House* by Reed Whittemore, copyright 1974 by Reed Whittemore is reprinted by permission of Houghton Mifflin Company.

"Beaucoup Buttercups" by Jonathan Williams is reprinted by permission of the author.

The poems of Miller Williams are reprinted by permission of the author and Louisiana State University Press.

"Some Applications of Certain Devices of Structural Linguistics to Prosody" first appeared in *The CEA Critic*. Copyright 1983 by Miller Williams.

"Some Observations on the Line" first appeared in *Antaeus*. Copyright 1979 by Miller Williams.

"Elegiac Stanza on a Photo of Ethel Rosenberg in Her Kitchen" by John A. Wood is reprinted by permission of the author. Copyright 1985 by John A. Wood.

Prefatory Note

Parts 1–3 present the poetic patterns in order of increasing length. Throughout the book, references to the patterns are in small capitals.

PATTERNS OF POETRY

Introduction: Form and the Age

It is in the nature of the arts—including literature—that they shape themselves to social changes, whether these are major upheavals altering the lives of a population in midcourse or slower shifts in the social climate, hardly perceptible to those who live through them. The French Revolution in the eighteenth century, the English Civil War and the Thirty Years' War in the seventeenth, and the Great Depression in the twentieth had profound effects on the arts; so did the westward expansion of the United States following the railroad over a period of 50 years or so, the colonizing of the New World over a period of 250, and the spread of Christianity over two millennia. All of the arts, those we call practical and those we call fine—architecture, dance, drama, literature, music, painting, sculpture, dress design, film—are ways we have of fitting social change to the contours of the human mind, while the mind, of course, is being shaped by such events. By this reciprocal play between what we are and what we do, we move in one direction for a period as that very movement builds the pressures that turn us in another. So we have histories, and so those histories have their periods. And every period makes its own patterns, shaping space and time for the eye and ear to the needs of a generation or a century.

How a form relates to the life of the age in which it emerges, or re-emerges, is among the central questions a student of the arts must explore. We can never, probably, say that there was a certain cause or set of causes that led Pope's generation to write in couplets or Wordsworth's generation to turn away from them. But we do know that when a given span of history is dominated by a way of responding to the world—which is to say a way of seeing and hearing and thinking—it eventually cuts across all areas of human expression. The imperatives that closed the later symphonies of Beethoven were fully as assured as Napoleon's. Theirs was a time in which affirmations

1

were appropriate and understood because they could be believed; they seemed for a while to be consistent with the nature of things.

Unqualified affirmations were not so easily accepted in the early Middle Ages, a time of social uncertainties created by feudalism—which at its heart is anarchistic—and nearly constant warfare. Artists had little confidence in the genius of their own time; architects were imitating the styles of ancient Rome as symbols of order and stability, while painters mixed Roman and Byzantine elements and borrowed what energy they could find in primitive Celtic influences. The painting of the early Middle Ages was for the most part apocalyptic; the prevailing vision of the human lot, though it affirmed God's existence and His active intervention in the life of mankind, was a dark one. If there was much yea-saying or much of the confidence that gives rise to adventure in the arts, evidence of it has not come down to us.

Eventually, after about seven hundred years, society began to put itself in order and the apocalyptic vision faded. The middle and late Middle Ages were characterized by strong central governments and confidence in the social order. A more songlike quality insinuated itself into ecclesiastical music, which previously had been very serious and often somber. Stained glass and painting both instructed and inspired, while church architecture, with tall, lean pillars, vaulted ceilings, and high, open spaces, seemed almost to defeat gravity. Poets invented small, lyrical patterns:

> Westron wind, when wilt thou blow?
> The small rain down can rain.
> Christ, that my love were in my arms,
> And I in my bed again.
>
> —Anonymous

Citizens of new nations in what we now call the Gothic period (about the twelfth through the fifteenth centuries) must have felt a new sense of worth and freedom as they became conscious of themselves. Through their poets and storytellers—Dante, Boccaccio, and Petrarch in Florentine and others in Northern Latian, Umbrian, Marchigiano, Roman, and other tongues in Italy and throughout Europe—they also became conscious of the languages they spoke, languages created as the vulgar Latin of departed soldiers and bureaucrats blended over centuries with native tongues. Those who have agreed with W. H. Auden's observation that poetry makes nothing happen might note that the power of language in the hands of the poets of Florence was greatly responsible for making Florentine the language of Italy.

The Church was the cohesive center that made division into states and languages possible without being ruinous, and all the arts—in fact, most public human activity—served it. The Gothic style marked the high point of the search for an art in which the faith of Christianity in its most joyous aspect could be fully manifest. It was manifest, appropriately, on a grand scale.

In the fifteenth century came the beginnings of the Renaissance, with the rediscovery of humanism in the work of such philosophers as Erasmus and, in painting and architecture, with a clarity, a calm, less ecstatic assurance, and a return to the human scale. As they had been in antiquity, forms were based on forms in nature. The arts came to be marked not by a faith in religion but by an almost religious faith in the power of the human mind to know the world. This was true in Italy in any case. The rest of Europe lagged behind by about a hundred years.

Inasmuch as one can speak of artists as a group, and recognizing that all the arts did not undergo the same developments simultaneously, one can say in general terms that artists at the height of the Renaissance wanted their works to suggest a serenity, a balance, and an order reflecting these very qualities of the natural world. Particularly good examples, for those who want to browse museums or art books, are Andrea del Castagno's *The Last Supper* and Piero della Francesca's *Resurrection of Christ*. Designers (which in the best sense all artists are) must always believe that their designs somehow reflect the world as it truly is.

So a rough folk dance of fifteenth-century France was adapted by the courts and transformed into the quietly lyrical, assured pavane. Poetry in English found this serenity in the increasingly stately lines of Sidney and then Spenser, Marlowe, and Shakespeare.

The moods of a culture are mercurial. Before the sixteenth century was past, artists such as the painter Il Bronzino and the sculptor Giovanni da Bologna were turning with others away from the attitudes and practices of the High Renaissance, which were mostly matters of consensus, to the individual expression of the minds of the artists, for this was again a time of tumult. The Protestant Reformation, French incursions into Italy, papal corruption, the sack of Rome in 1527, and other traumas suffered by structure made consensus no longer possible and gave rise to a pessimism about the nature of the world. This was the Age of Mannerism, an age that, as Kenneth Clark has put it in his *Civilization*, lost faith "in the decency and high destiny" of humanity and took as its motto "play it for kicks"—an attitude not wholly foreign to some later times. In poetry, mannerism ultimately found its expression in the verses of the cavalier poets of England, such as Thomas Carew, Richard Lovelace, and John Suckling.

When that ironically pessimistic and playful period spent itself into exhaustion, it was followed by a reemergence of religious orientation in the arts and a weakening of humanism as a way of viewing life. This new vision, perhaps best typified in English verse by Crashaw, was marked by the fantastic and discordant, the unexpected, all playing upon a hard realism and logic, an admixture not far removed from the Magic Realism originating in twentieth-century Latin American literature. The forms of all the arts in this phase of our passage, which we now call the baroque period (roughly from the later sixteenth to the early eighteenth centuries), were irrational, emotional, serious, elaborate, and marked by a contorted opulence. The shift in sensibility became manifest in such works as the later poems of John Donne and the major poems of Milton. Among the master painters of the period were Caravaggio, Carracci, Hals, Rembrandt, and Velázquez; the major sculptor was Bernini. In the court, the pavane shared the floor with the galliard, a highly emotional dance of almost uncontrollable but intricate frenzy.

The response of a culture to any pressure impinging upon it, baroque or romantic or whatever, has the energy of originality only so long as the original pressure is there. When the pressure dissipates, a younger generation that never knew it firsthand will continue to do as their parents and grandparents did, with inertia as their only energy. So every movement falls into decadence until a few artists begin to recognize new pressures and respond to them.

So in the eighteenth century the baroque gave way to the rococo, a style in which the powerful outpouring of emotions represented by the baroque was restrained, first to an elegant refinement and then to a lyrical sentimentality. Delicately ornate decorations replaced the massive elements of baroque buildings, and in music the wit of Grazioli and Rutini took over programs previously dedicated wholly to the exuberance of Monteverdi, the Scarlattis, Vivaldi, Corelli, Bach, Handel, and their baroque contemporaries.

The only dance to dance was the minuet. It was a courtly dance of slow elegance and grace, influenced by the also widely popular ballet. It had, like the pavane, been a dance of the streets and countryside before the aristocracy took it indoors to make it the symbol of a ceremonial society, *i.e.*, a society in which, among the ruling class, the simplest social exchange was stylized. All the world was indeed a stage, and the powdered wigs and heavy face paint were marvelously appropriate.

Poetry in English during this period was for the most part an exercise in wit (Pope's *Rape of the Lock*, Gay's *Fan*), but some poetry, such as Pope's *Essay on Man*, responded by opposing the prevalent direction of society rather than endorsing it and became moral and satiric in its longer forms, as in Dryden's *Mac Flecknoe*. The writers of the short lyric, a form that had flowered in the Renaissance with verses of great distinction, began to turn out easy, conventional verses like Matthew Prior's "A Better Answer."

> Dear Cloe, how blubbered is that pretty face!
> Thy cheek all on fire, and thy hair all uncurled!
> Prithee quit this caprice; and (as old Falstaff says)
> Let us e'en talk a little like folks of this world.

There began to develop by the beginning of the eighteenth century an interest in a wider range of expression than gaiety and energy, a more inquiring art. The French Revolution in the last decade of the century made this the only legitimate interest, as it demanded a rejection of eighteenth-century attitudes. It might be closer to the truth to say that a more inquiring art was the only legitimate interest when people were not dancing, for the waltz became a craze at the end of the century, a double-dactylic, joyful experience of liberation, breaking resolutely away from the proscriptions of the minuet and the philosophy inherent in the minuet, which had emphasized a pattern of order and reason overseen by a sovereign, the individual submerged in the pattern.

As that segment of the earth's population we very loosely call the

Western world entered the nineteenth century, then, imagination replaced reason as the noblest of human faculties, and romanticism held sway as the expression of it and as the expression of that nationalism to which romanticism is so often wedded. It found its home not only in the musical dramas of Wagner and the works of Chopin and Brahms, but also in the revolts of the Czechs against the Turks and of the Poles against the Russians.

Although most scholars agree that in the final analysis Beethoven never was a committed romantic (he was as stubborn, daring, and innovative as any but was also regularly pragmatic and classical), he nevertheless was a man of his age. One mark of his age that he exemplified as surely as any man did was a belief in the ideal and the heroic; another was a fierce and certain faith in the truth of his own vision. What can the unqualified assertion of those final chords say but "amen"? How many can say the same today, to any vision, without feeling dishonest?

Still, we can in our age hear Beethoven's "amen" and find a joy in the hearing of it; we can enjoy the harpsichord, knowing that even with the attendant skills we could not write for it. It was perfect for the clear, unambiguous assertions of the early eighteenth century, but the piano was required for the rambling passions of romanticism. When we enjoy the harpsichord now, we listen with a historical imagination. So do we also when we enjoy Beethoven in his turn, and Milton in his.

In the latter half of the nineteenth century, the Industrial Revolution and the technology that accompanied it, reinforced by revolutionary social and scientific views, scattered the Western world's poets and painters, architects and dancers, and composers and sculptors as they had never been scattered before. Some looked for shelter from the questions being thrown at them out of the burgeoning smokestacks and the mouths of Marx and Freud and Darwin. Some, like the Pre-Raphaelites, went back to the past to known patterns and responses. Some, like the impressionists, looked for new ones in a private, subjective experience of softened perceptions. In France, Baudelaire responded with *Les Fleurs du Mal*, Valéry wrote *Le Cimetière Marin*, and Mallarmé disregarded syntax and led his friends into the protective maze of symbolism. In the United States, Whitman sang of himself. In painting, the Fauves—the "wild beasts," so called as a slur by the critic Louis Vauxcelles—had introduced themselves as early as 1905 in an exhibition of their pictures in Paris. The violence they did to the accustomed sense of harmony in color and form outraged those who came to look and opened the door to what we call the modern period. It was as if the end of the Renaissance were being played out all over again, with no Renaissance to look back on. The scattered never returned to a consensus, except at times to the common view that what was past was suspect.

For well over a hundred years the arts have survived without consensus, except as fragments from an explosion move in concert away from the center. Theater-in-the-round, break dancing, jazz, rock, abstract expressionism in painting and architecture, and abstract poetry all are manifestations of our reaction to the shattering of common sureties in the mid-nineteenth century and the diaspora that followed.

There have been fads and some surges of interest almost worth calling movements, but no prevailing direction. In poetry there has been imagism, modernism, projectivism, postmodernism, beat poetry, confessional poetry, academic poetry, concrete poetry, the New Poetry, the poetry of the Fugitives, and the poetry of Yvor Winters and his students. At least these. Some—the academics (sons and daughters of the Fugitives) and Yvor Winters and his disciples—suggested that a confrontation with the future required a dialogue with the past, but in great part, poets over the past hundred years have busied themselves with not looking back, with being free of what was to be seen there.

Looking back anyway, as we have—given that this skimming of a thousand years is, in the kindest judgment, simplistic—we see that it makes little sense to divide the human experience into a past and a present. There are many kinds of past. Our present is, this moment, taking its place as one of them, and future poets will mine it for what is useful. Our parts are distinguishable one from the other, but they are parts of an unbreakable continuum, like the seasons of the years. And we see that our history keeps turning around to meet itself. We cannot assume, then, that the past is behind us; it may, in a slightly altered form, lie waiting ahead of us. In fact, it almost surely does. The very mercurial nature of our culture cautions us to be unsure of the emotional, if not the rational, substance we stand on.

Because we associate a sensibility with an age, we sometimes fall prey to the misconception that a sensibility and the forms associated with it properly and wholly disappear when the epoch dominated by that sensibility is past. The fact is that a way of responding to the world, once learned by the human race, is never wholly unlearned or useless. For that matter, rarely if ever is a way of seeing and thinking totally new.

We speak of a revolution that gave us modern poetry, for instance, but such a revolution never came to pass. Victorian poetry did not become modern poetry out of nothing, with the turning of a calendar page, as impressionist painting did not give way to postimpressionism one New Year's Day. We do not walk out of one age and into another. We never, in fact, leave the past. As Browning and Donne were already "modern," so we—if we are complete—still live partly in the nineteenth and seventeenth centuries.

A particular attitude and set of responses may seem almost to disappear, but they will rise up again, as we have seen—always in altered forms—to hold minds in thrall, as the expressionist movement in painting at the beginning of the twentieth century, with its emphasis on subjective experience and suggestions of the transcendental, manifested the same sensibility that informed baroque art in the sixteenth. And as skepticism—not in the sense of pessimism or necessarily religious doubt—took hold of the minds of the Greek disciples of Pyrrho of Elis, of the nominalists and mystics of the Middle Ages, of the circle of Montaigne in the sixteenth century, of the followers of Pascal in the seventeenth, of the eighteenth-century neoclassicists, and of the nineteenth-century romantics. The pessimism that marked the Age of Mannerism in the sixteenth century shows up again in the work of some of the Pre-Raphaelites and Oscar Wilde in the mid-nineteenth century and of some of the dadaists in the early twentieth.

History is not linear; rather, its progress describes something like a helix. We come back to the plane we were in before, but not at the same place. Poetry has changed, certainly. The furniture of the world has changed, but nothing has passed out of existence in the realms of the mind. We may speak in the detached and reportorial voice of classicism or the prophetic and passionate voice of romanticism, but we know a well-turned line in either voice. A good poem lives in its own time and speaks to all times. Poems written before the Industrial Revolution were not at their centers expressions of horses and water-wheels; they were expressions of human beings, and we do not change very much, whatever the mood of a generation may be. We are still concerned mostly with love and sex, death and loss, religion and awe, and ambition.

People who talk about poetry in English, especially those who get paid to talk about it, generally will say that modern poetry is marked in style by freedom, in tone by forthrightness, and in content by relevance to our immediate concerns. They will say that we recognize it by open forms—*i.e.*, the absence of strict patterns—and by slant and irregular (if any) rhyme, conversational language, and treatment of likely human situations. This is fair, but many of the best poems of our tradition spoke so naturally in this world's voice, about things so mundane and essential to ordinary people, that we can still hear those voices as almost ours. I think for instance of Thomas Wyatt's "They flee from me, that sometime did me seek. . . ." There are some quaint conventions in the diction, naturally, but how contemporary Wyatt is in his figures, his tone, and his interest, after more than four hundred years.

> In thin array, after a pleasant guise,
> When her loose gown from her shoulders did fall,
> And she caught me in her arms long and small,
> And therewith all sweetly did me kiss
> And softly said, "Dear heart, how like you this?"

And this is not to mention the voices and subjects of Chaucer and Burns and Browning and many other good poets from every age.

I have addressed the question of tone, diction, and content in a discussion of patterns because many poets and readers associate patterns with what they take to be the too-artful tone, language, and interests of the past. This is especially true of those poets writing today who have assumed the heavy cloak of romanticism, whose philosophy and poems are informed by a reverence for what they see as the natural, the plain, even the primitive, for spontaneity, for a universal oneness that denies the divisions of genre, for distrust of the rational and the devised. It is not surprising that these poets dislike the elements of artifact that make poetry seem invented and that emphasize the distinctions between verse and prose. It is unfortunate that they have

sometimes politicized the question of form, seeing patterns themselves as a manifestation of reactionary sympathies, and unpatterned
poetry as the work of a politically liberated mind. This rises, perhaps,
from an interpretation of the term *free verse* to mean "free from the
bonds of tradition," but whatever the source of the misapprehension,
we should be disabused of it, for it deprives poems of a richness of
texture that even the remnant memory of traditional patterns may lend.

The word *liberated* takes on a note of irony in this context, for the
successful rebel often becomes the new arbiter of behavior, establishment replaces establishment, and the new dispensation becomes as
proscriptive as the old. We live in a time of putative freedom to write,
and to dress, more or less as one likes, but if there is a social and ultimately a political pressure to express that freedom in a certain way, it
is no longer freedom. The freedom not to wear a tie is an illusion unless there is also freedom to wear one.

The disdain for patterns is in fact a disdain for the past itself, a kind
of temporal chauvinism, born surely of misperceptions about both
form and language. But it is in the matter of form that we are most
likely to find distinctions made between modern poetry and what has
preceded it, and to slip into the flattering assumption that we have
been doing something essentially new. Free verse, we are given to
understand, is modern; earlier poetry was not free. It had patterns.

Free verse is a label we give to a poetical work in which a reader is
unable to predict from foregoing lines or from tradition the length of
the next line or the position or nature of the next rhyme, if one occurs.
What are we to make, then, of Milton's "Lycidas," a poem that dates
from 1637? Most of it is set in pentameter, but trimeter and tetrameter
lines intrude with no discernible pattern, and there is no pattern to
the rhyming. Built into the poem are stanzas of ottava rima, heroic
quatrains, heroic couplets, split couplet variations, and ten unrhymed
lines.

"Lycidas" does not seem like free verse to us, and we would be
foolish to call it that, in the common usage of the term. But one might
argue that it is not a formal poem, either, in the common usage of that
term. It may be fair to ask at what point a reader could say, "I see the
pattern here." The good fact is that we are not obliged to set formal
forever against free. Many admirable poems, like "Lycidas" and

George Herbert's "The Collar" and Eliot's "The Lovesong of J. Alfred Prufrock," have something of both about them.

It has been said to the point of banality that form should follow content. Edmund Spenser reached deeper to say the same thing in "An Hymn in Honor of Beauty":

> Of the soul the body form doth take;
> For soul is form, and doth the body make.

We have never pulled free of that dualism to see that neither form nor content shapes the other, that surely they must shape one another, like a river and its banks. This may rightly bring some poems to no containing frame, others to a loose and bending frame, and others to the strictest of forms, while the voices within them remain voices of our place in time and on the earth.

The differences between a poem written well today and a well-written poem from the past are sharper when we compare our poetry to some periods—say, the neoclassical or romantic—than to others—as for instance the period of Chaucer or of the late medieval lyrics or of the early seventeenth century. But it is all a single growth, and the roots are still felt in the branches.

So if there is little that is new, there is also little that is old, in the sense that we are through with it. A part of the good fortune of poetry in English is that while we can find poets in nearly every period of the past doing what we mostly do, we can also write, when we find it useful, as they mostly did, in strict or modified sonnets and villanelles and sestinas and ballad stanzas. If we have not invented very much, neither have we lost very much.

Strict patterns, used consistently, would probably not be suitable to the public voice or private vision of many poets writing today, though some—Anthony Hecht, X. J. Kennedy, Philip Larkin, James Whitehead, and Richard Wilbur, to name five—do use them both consistently and convincingly, and Dylan Thomas chose the strictest forms to contain his most violent images. Perhaps more important to the present generation of poets is the way in which these patterns, allowed to be a little more resilient, followed not so rigorously, can inform new poems in such a manner that a sonnet or villanelle or sestina is not written but suggested. This is the allusory pattern, and it has its own uses: it stirs old associations, as allusion will, and it surprises our expectations by being not finally the form it reminds us of. And even the suggestion of one of the forms, when a poet understands it well, can haunt a good poem like a ghost.

Notes on the Elements of Poetic Forms

RHYME AND OTHER ECHOES. Two words whose sounds echo one another may be akin by rhyme, assonance, consonance, or alliteration. Assonance and consonance are now generally treated together as slant rhyme, off rhyme, or half rhyme, but the effects differ markedly and the distinction should not be lost.

By definition: *Rhyme* is the relationship between words with different consonants immediately preceding the final accented vowels and identical sounds thereafter (pillow/willow, go/know, undoing/construing). *Assonance* is the relationship between words with different consonants immediately preceding and following the last accented vowels, which vowels have identical sounds (hit/will, disturb/bird, absolute/unglued). *Consonance* is the relationship between words whose final accented vowel sounds are different but with the same consonant frame (truck/trick, billion/bullion, impelling/compiling, trance/trounce). *Alliteration* is the relationship between words with identical consonants preceding the first accented vowel and differing sounds on that vowel, on the subsequent consonant, if any, and possibly, but not necessarily, on all following sounds (slip/slide, glowing/glare). It may be useful to look at them as they are presented in the table on the following page.

Anyone with more than a casual interest in the nature and effects of sound play in poetry should read Wilfred Owen's "Strange Meeting" to see consonance as it has rarely if ever been put to work elsewhere. The poetry of Emily Dickinson is an education in the use of assonance. The Anglo-Saxon poetry in this volume offers a good sampling of alliteration. True rhyme is used throughout the book in the great majority of poems.

As assonance and consonance are subtler phonic kinships than pure rhyme, they themselves have softer expressions in the vocalic echo and the consonantal echo, respectively. *Vocalic echo* is a relation-

NAME	EXAMPLE	CONSONANTS IMMEDIATELY BEFORE LAST ACCENTED VOWEL	LAST ACCENTED VOWEL	CONSONANTS IMMEDIATELY FOLLOWING LAST ACCENTED VOWEL
Rhyme	pillow/willow	different	same	same (and all sounds following)
Assonance	hit/will	different	same	different
Consonance	lip/lap	same	different	same (and all sounds following)
Alliteration	slip/slow	same	different	different (and possibly all sounds following)

ship between two words in which vowel sounds are repeated but not necessarily in order (cotillion/billygoat). *Consonantal echo* is a relationship between two words in which consonant sounds, stressed or unstressed, are repeated, but not, as in alliteration, in the same order (tell/late, falter/traffic).

THE PROSODIC SYMBOLS

- ⏑ An unaccented syllable
- / An accented syllable
- s A syllable in a syllabic poem
- x A nonrhyming line
- a (or any small unaccented letter except x or s). A rhyming line
- *or* A prescribed (not an accidental) off rhyme
- A (or any capital letter). A refrain. Tradition allows for some varying of a refrain, especially when the change adds something to the statement the poem is making or the story it tells. A "growth" in the refrain throughout the poem, as when each refrain takes us farther west or farther up or simply becomes longer,

is called *incremental repetition, i.e.,* "It is midnight now in Samoa"; then, "It is midnight now in Osaka"; then, "It is midnight now in Djakarta," etc.

A_1, A_2 (or any capital letters with subscripts). Different refrains that rhyme with one another

á   (or any accented small letter). A repeated end word

Aá   (or any such combination). A new refrain ending with the end word of an earlier refrain

‖   A *caesura*—a break in the movement, a pause in a line (or at the end of a line, though the term is generally reserved for in-line pauses, while a line with a pause at the end is said to be *end-stopped*). Sometimes (see POULTER'S MEASURE) syntactic breaks, though not "heard," may satisfy the call for a caesura in a verse pattern. In Greek and Latin this generally fell in the middle of the third or fourth foot. In contemporary English poetry it falls anywhere near the middle of the line, sometimes coinciding with a half foot.

For an example of how the prosodic symbols are used to indicate a poem's rhymes and measures, we can look at "Triolet," by Robert Bridges, and the annotation for it.

When first we met we did not guess
That Love would prove so hard a master;
Of more than common friendliness
When first we met we did not guess.
Who could foretell this sore distress
This irretrievable disaster
When first we met?—We did not guess
That love would prove so hard a master.

MEASURE				RHYME
◡ /	◡ /	◡ /	◡ /	A
◡ /	◡ /	◡ /	◡ / ◡	B
◡ /	◡ /	◡ /	◡ /	a
◡ /	◡ /	◡ /	◡ /	A
/ ◡	◡ /	◡ /	◡ /	a
◡ /	◡ /	◡ /	◡ / ◡	b
◡ /	◡ /	◡ /	◡ /	A
◡ /	◡ /	◡ /	◡ / ◡	B

Note how the reversal of the first foot in line 5 increases interest by introducing variety and a greater sense of the human voice while at the same time adding increased emphasis to the important word *who*. The reversal of a foot or the substitution of one foot for another (this is actually, of course, the exchange of a trochee for the iamb) will always underscore the word or syllable receiving the accent out of order. A formal poem of more than a few lines with no such substitution is likely to sound excessively metronomic and become monotonous. Note also the added syllables at the ends of three of the lines. (See HYPERMETER in Glossary.)

POULTER'S MEASURE, which includes a caesura, may be written and annotated in this way (remembering that the caesura may, as in line 1, be syntactic only, but is usually—as in line 3—"heard" as a pause):

> But ye whom love hath found by order of desire
> to love your lords, whose good deserts none other would require,
> Come ye once again and set your foot by mine,
> whose woeful plight and sorrows great no tongue can ever define.
>
> —Henry Howard, Earl of Surrey

MEASURE							RHYME
‿∕	‿∕	‿∕	‖	‿∕	‿∕	‿∕	a
‿∕	‿∕	‿∕	‿∕	‿∕	‿∕	‿∕	a
‿∕	‿∕	‿∕	‖	‿∕	‿∕	‿∕	b
‿∕	‿∕	‿∕	‿∕	‿∕	‿∕	‿∕	b

THE MAJOR FEET

NAME	SYMBOL	SOURCE
Iamb	‿∕	Unknown
Pyrrhus	‿‿	From a step in an ancient Greek war dance, after Pyrrhichus, the inventor of the dance.
Spondee	∕∕	The Greek word for a solemn toast, suggesting the slow, serious music that was meant to accompany such an event. The heaviness of the adjacent strong beats in the spondee is usually

NAME	SYMBOL	SOURCE
		compensated for by a foregoing or following pyrrhic foot, creating an ionic foot.
Trochee	/ ◡	From the Greek for "to run (trippingly)"
Amphibrach	◡ / ◡	From the Greek for "short on both sides"
Anapest	◡◡ /	From the Greek for "to hit back"
Bacchic foot	◡ / /	After a dominant beat in the odes to Bacchus
Antibacchic foot	/ / ◡	The opposite of the bacchic foot
Cretic foot	/ ◡ /	From a dominant beat in the poetry of Crete
Dactyl	/ ◡◡	From the Latin for "finger" (suggesting the three joints)
Ionic (major)	/ / ◡◡	A spondee followed by a pyrrhus
Ionic (minor)	◡◡ / /	A pyrrhus followed by a spondee

METRICS. The set acoustic pattern of a line of poetry is its *meter*. The study of meter is called *metrics* or *prosody*. A line may be measured by its syllables, its accented syllables, or both. That is, it may be *syllabic* (with a fixed number of syllables per line), *accentual* (with a fixed number of stresses per line), or *accentual-syllabic* (with both the syllable count and stress count fixed). In English, the accentual-syllabic line has traditionally been the preferred one, and it still informs the great majority of our formal poems.

The lines of HYMNAL MEASURE will do as well as any for an example.

	SYLLABLES	STRESSES
O God, our Help in ages past	8	4
Our Hope for years to come,	6	3
Our Shelter from the stormy blast,	8	4
And our eternal Home.	6	3

—Isaac Watts

	SYLLABLES	STRESSES
A slumber did my spirit seal;	8	4
I had no human fears:	6	3

	SYLLABLES	STRESSES
She seemed a thing that could not feel	8	4
The touch of earthly years.	6	3

—William Wordsworth

Since both syllable count and foot count are regular, and since a foot always represents a determined number of stresses, these lines are accurately referred to as accentual-syllabic, as are those that follow.

	SYLLABLES	STRESSES
Said a mythical king of Algiers;	9	3

—Anonymous, from a limerick

	SYLLABLES	STRESSES
The world is too much with us; late and soon,	10	5
Getting and spending, we lay waste our powers;	10	5

—Wordsworth, from a sonnet

Michael Heffernan's "The Whereabouts" is based on syllable count alone; the lines vary in their number of accents, since no attention is paid to the nature or number of feet.

	SYLLABLES	STRESSES
Whenever he found himself there, whenever	11	5
he was at large and his whereabouts unknown,	11	5
with someone trying to find him—say the wife	11	5
or the man from the credit-card company	11	4
or the cops—though he never did anything	11	5
and was never the kind of person that did;	11	4
whenever, in short, he was ever wanted	11	5
to make an appearance or come into view	11	4
for whatever reason, he was never there	11	5
not ever in one place where you could find him.	11	5

You will notice that even though the poet gave no thought to metrical regularity, most of the lines have five stresses and break down into accidental iambs and anapests. This is an all but unavoidable function of the natural rhythms of the English language, and the reason that many readers question the efficacy of the syllabic line in English. The measure is standard in French, an unaccented language in which stress count cannot override syllabic measure.

In accentual poetry, only stresses per line count as a measure of the line's length. Compare Edward FitzGerald's version of Omar Khayyám's RUBAIYAT form, which is strictly accentual-syllabic, to my own accentual use of the form.

	SYLLABLES	STRESSES
The Moving Finger writes and having writ	10	5
Moves on; nor all your Piety nor Wit	10	5
Shall lure it back to cancel half a Line	10	5
Nor all your Tears wash out a Word of it.	10	5
Sue Ella Tucker was barely in her teens.	11	5
She often minded her mother. She didn't know beans	13	5
About what boys can do. She laughed like air.	10	5
Already the word was crawling up her jeans	11	5

Note that (again, in the nature of English) most of the feet in the accentual verse are iambs and that nearly all of the rest are anapests. The fact is that the English line tends so strongly to accentual-syllabics that accentuals and syllabics will move toward that middle form.

In this book the patterns will be defined by their traditional measures, which in nearly every case will mean accentual-syllabics, but it should be borne in mind that among many contemporary poets there has been some "softening" of the patterns from accentual-syllabics to accentuals.

The illusion of conversation, and of its sense of immediacy and relevance, is enhanced by increasingly casual metrics and by the absence or softening of rhyme, as each of these will at the same time lessen the sense of ritual upon which all art depends. We pay for one with the other and we need them both. William Meredith has caught a balance in that tension in the following lines. They all have five stresses but no established foot, and they vary from ten syllables to thirteen; they are all rhymed but (with the exception of one pair of words) rhymed slant. We can see some of the effects of accentuals and of slant rhyme if we compare this poem, which is composed of SICILIAN QUATRAINS, to the two stricter examples on p. 44.

ABOUT OPERA

It's not the tunes, although as I get older
Arias are what I hum and whistle.
It's not the plots—they continue to bewilder
In the tongue I speak and in several that I wrestle.

An image of articulateness is what it is:
Isn't this how we've always longed to talk?
Words as they fall are monotone and bloodless
But they yearn to take the risk these noises take.

What dancing is to the slightly spastic way
Most of us teeter through our bodily life
Are these measured cries to the clumsy things we say,
In the heart's duresses, on the heart's behalf.

        —William Meredith

NONCE FORMS. Many poems are written in patterns invented by the poet, which are called *nonce forms*. The adjective is derived by misdivision from the medieval phrase "for then anes," meaning "for then once," or "for the one time." By the Renaissance this had become "for the nonce," and so a poetic form devised for a single poem was a form "for the nonce," or a nonce form. All the traditional patterns of poetry were once nonce forms.

Although we should imagine a very shadowy line between formal and informal poetry, nonce forms do not exist in that realm. The following three poems move progressively into it, so they are not really nonce forms, though the sequence of line length and rhyme in each is invented. Rhyme or line or both lack sufficient regularity to make possible a prediction of what is to come next.

This is not to denigrate the poems, which are quite convincing. William Mills, in fact, has demonstrated particularly well the charm that a softened and flexible formal frame may give a poem, as suggested in the Introduction.

GRANNY DEAN

Each spring,
Even when she'd slipped

Past eighty, she scrapped
Her winter drapes
And came out with the green.
Rare the day she wasn't seen
Where wild things bloom,
Time-sprung hands routing daisies
For her small room.

—Alvin Aubert

BREAD

There are many ways to live. Whole wheat
is tasty, so are rye and white

and sesame, oatmeal, acorn, maize,
bread tanning forever on trays

of dawn—in factories
and towns, on farms at first light,

even the settled hermit waking
breaks it again, this common thing.

As for me, I'd say one loaf
a day could be enough:

bread for your morning visit, bread
and honey, or bread with tea and marmalade.

Let nobody go wanting, and let the grain
be fresh and broken by the moving sun.

—Jonathan Aldrich

WINTER STELE

You have decided marrying won't do.
I could have been the many to your one
And you to me. Instead the world darkens to your kiss.
Rather than cross long love's Rubicon
You chose to stay and be quick pleasure's nun.

Now we stand like straight sticks
That add to nothing, never a home,

Now remain like winter stele of an undone spring
Where people come to ritual and ghosts, to beg and atone.
See us, see us stand, alone and alone.

—William Mills

The pattern of William Meredith's "The Couple Overhead" is a nonce form. The lines are set in a loose but regular three-stress accentual measure; the rhyme pattern is as elegantly devised as the measure is casual.

THE COUPLE OVERHEAD

They don't get anywhere,	a
The couple overhead;	b
They wrangle like the damned	c
In the bed above my bed,	b
But the harm has all been done.	d
And this is a short despair:	a
Count Ugolino dead	b
Was endlessly condemned	c
To gnaw the archbishop's head	b
Where the nape and skull are one.	d
Not so, these secular drunks.	e
Dante would find their treason	f
Too spiritless to keep;	g
Like children stealing raisins	f
They eat each other's eyes;	h
The ice that grips their flanks	e
Is something they have frozen.	f
After a while they sleep;	g
And the punishment they've chosen,	f
After a while it dies.	h

—William Meredith

1 🖋 Fully Defined Traditional Stanza Patterns

SHORT COUPLET. Probably English in origin. Two rhymed lines, traditionally iambic or trochaic tetrameter. As in the case of many formal poems, the pattern is "softened" by the reversal of feet, as when a trochee (/ ◡) is substituted for an iamb (◡ /), and by *catalexis* (the omission of an unaccented syllable).

```
◡ /    ◡ /    ◡ /    ◡ /        a
◡ /    ◡ /    ◡ /    ◡ /        a
```

JANUARY: A FLIGHT OF BIRDS

Watching the birds, I think of Bach,
each of the distant wheeling flock

a black note on a turning page,
the darkened afternoon the stage.

Watching their wide, then narrow belt
I imagine how Bach felt,

with hundreds of melodies all at once,
inventing his own celestial stunts.

In their equivalent of cantata,
the birds perform a short fermata

then in silent sky-bound bugle
swoop and go, their music fugal.

I think of their flight in terms of Master
Bach at his keyboard, writing vaster

harmonies than the court could dream—
which is why, in pure esteem,

the world would be if Bach- and bird-less,
as much diminished as if wordless.

—John Stone

EPITAPH FOR GOLIATH

After so many victories, one
defeat, and that one by a stone:
but let this stone atone for that
breach of the order of combat.
He was a victim of a ruse
of the rude boy of the barbarous Jews.
Goliath shall have honor while
men yet have any use for style
or the purity of form they mean
by the accolade of Philistine.

—David Slavitt

SPLIT COUPLET. Probably English in origin. Two rhymed lines; one
of five stresses followed by one of two stresses, traditionally iambic.

$\cup$ / $\cup$ / $\cup$ / $\cup$ / $\cup$ /   a
$\cup$ / $\cup$ /   a

LINES AT FOUR IN THE MORNING

A book is coming out I wrote somehow.
I could not now.

The new Buck Rogers bores me. I prefer
the way things were

in rocket ships of my youth. So I look,
book by book,

forward toward my past, as also I'm
(to bend time

further out of shape) nostalgic about
the future. I doubt

this sort of thing is good to think a lot.
Probably not.

—Clement Long

SKELTONIC COUPLET. Named for John Skelton (*ca.* 1460–1529), who popularized it. Generally considered English in origin but probably timeless. Two rhymed lines, traditionally iambic, most often two or three feet in length. Sometimes marked by a deliberately metronomic beat and audacious rhyme. Written as complete, aphoristic poems, these are termed *didactic* or *primer* couplets because of their use in early readers ("In Adam's fall / We sinnéd all").

```
∪ /    ∪ /        a
∪ /    ∪ /        a
```

UPON A DEAD MAN'S HEAD

Your ugly token
My mind hath broken
From worldly lust;
For I have discussed
We are but dust,
And die we must.
    It is general
To be mortal:
I have well espied
No man may him hide
From Death hollow-eyed,
With sinews wyderëd,
With bones shyderëd,
With his worm-eaten maw,
And his ghastly jaw
Gasping aside,
Naked of hide,
Neither flesh nor fell.
    Then, by my counsel,
Look that ye spell
Well this gospel:

For whereso we dwell
Death will us quell
And with us mell.
   For all our pampered paunches
There may no fraunchis,
Nor worldly bliss,
Redeem us from this:
Our days be dated
To be checkmated
With draughtës of death
Stopping our breath:
Our eyen sinking,
Our bodies stinking,
Our gummës grinning,
Our soulës brinning.
To whom, then, shall we sue,
For to have rescue,
But to sweet Jesu
On us then for to rue?

   O goodly Child
Of Mary mild,
Then be our shield!
That we be not exiled
To the dyne dale
Of bootless bale,
Nor to the lake
Of fiendës black.
   But grant us grace
To see thy Face,
And to purcháse
Thine heavenly place,
And thy paláce
Full of soláce
Above the sky
That is so high:
Eternally

To behold and see
The Trinity!
   Amen.

            —John Skelton

HEROIC COUPLET. English in origin. Two rhymed lines of five stresses each, traditionally iambic, often with a full stop at the end of each stanza. Most epics—*i.e.*, heroic poems—in English were written in iambic pentameter, so that all forms built on iambic pentameter are properly referred to as *heroic*. That is to say, iambic pentameter is the *heroic line*.

  ᴗ /   ᴗ /   ᴗ /   ᴗ /   ᴗ /   a
  ᴗ /   ᴗ /   ᴗ /   ᴗ /   ᴗ /   a

From ESSAY ON MAN

Vice is a monster of so frightful mien
As, to be hated, needs but to be seen;
Yet seen too oft, familiar with her face,
We first endure, then pity, then embrace.

            —Alexander Pope

In the following lines, the poet is satirizing what he sees as prevalent attitudes among his contemporaries. The book-length poem from which the lines are taken is patterned after Alexander Pope's long satire entitled *The Dunciad*. The "He" of the poem is the poet whose mind and work are the object of the satire.

From THE NARCISSIAD

Instead of reverence from the future ages
He dreams instead in terms of tabloid pages,
This quarter's final word on Love and Beauty
And, after that, to teach the dog his duty.
Confident in his art, he knows he's great
Because his subsidy comes from the State
For teaching self-expression to the masses

In jails, nut-houses; worse, in high-school classes
In which his sermon is (his poems show it)
That *anyone* can learn to be a poet.
With Flair in hand he takes the poet's stance
To write, instead of sonnets, sheaves of grants
Which touch the bureaucrats and move their hearts
To turn the spigot on and flood the arts
With cold cash, carbon copies, calculators,
And, for each poet, two administrators.
In brief, his every effort at creation
Is one more act of self-perpetuation
To raise the towering babble of his Reputation.

—R. S. Gwynn

ELEGIAC COUPLET. Classical in origin. Two lines, traditionally un-rhymed. As generally adapted from the classical measures, the lines are heard as dactylic hexameter, with line 1 lacking the second un-accented syllable in the third and sixth feet (*i.e.,* with trochaic sub-stitutions on those feet), and with the same feet in line 2 lacking both unaccented syllables. The second line is more properly described as pentameter composed of two dactyls, a split spondee (*i.e.,* with the two syllables separated by a caesura), and two anapests, as is shown by the foot divisions. The caesura, in both lines, is established in the pattern.

/ ᴗᴗ   / ᴗᴗ   / ᴗ   ‖   / ᴗᴗ   / ᴗᴗ   / ᴗ
/ ᴗᴗ   / ᴗᴗ   /   ‖   / ᴗᴗ   / ᴗᴗ   /

FOR VICTOR JARA

Mutilated and Murdered
The Soccer Stadium
Santiago, Chile

This is to say we remember. Not that remembering saves us.
Not that remembering brings anything usable back.

This is to say that we never have understood how to say this.
Out of our long unbelief what do we say to belief?

Nobody wants you to be there asking the question you ask us.
There had been others before, people who stayed to the end:

Utah and Boston and Memphis, Newgate, Geneva, Morelos—
Changing the sounds of those names, they have embarrassed us, too.

What shall we do with the stillness, do with the hate and the pity?
What shall we do with the love? What shall we do with the grief?

Such are the things that we think of, far from the thought that you
    hung there,
Silver inside of our heads, golden inside of our heads:

Would we have stayed to an end or would we have folded our faces?
Awful and awful. Good Friend. You have embarrassed our hearts.

—Miller Williams

POULTER'S MEASURE. English in origin. So called because with its thirteen feet it suggests the poulter's old practice of giving an extra egg with the second dozen. Two rhymed lines of six and seven feet respectively, traditionally iambic, with a central pause in line 1. See the note on the caesura on p. 15. Similar in effect to SHORT MEASURE, into which it tends to break up in the reading.

   ᴗ /   ᴗ /   ᴗ / || ᴗ /   ᴗ /   ᴗ /   a
   ᴗ /   ᴗ /   ᴗ /   ᴗ /   ᴗ /   ᴗ /   ᴗ /   a

Good ladies, ye that have your pleasures in exile,
Step in your foot, come take a place and mourn with me a while;
And such as by their lords do set but little price,
Let them sit still, it skills them not what chance come on the dice.
But ye whom love hath bound by order of desire
To love your lords, whose good desserts none other would require,
Come ye yet once again and set your foot by mine,
Whose woeful plight and sorrows great no tongue can well define.

—Henry Howard, Earl of Surrey

ENGLYN PENFYR (eng'-lin pen'-vir). Welsh in origin. A triplet built on rhyming on lines of ten, seven, and seven syllables. In the first line, this rhyme is buried up to three syllables back from the end of the line, the closing sound of which is echoed by true or slant rhyme at or near the beginning of line 2. This is best shown by setting the rhyme sounds into the scansion of the verse.

```
sssssssassb
bsssssa
ssssssa
```

The refrain in the following example is the poet's invention, not pre-scribed by the form.

THE CORPSE OF URIEN

The handsome corpse is laid down today,
Laid under this earth and stone—
Curse my fist! Owain's sire slain!

The handsome corpse is now broken
In the earth, under the oak—
Curse my fist! My kinsman struck!

The handsome corpse is bereft at last,
Fast in the stone he is left—
Curse my fist! My fate is cleft!

The handsome corpse is rewarded thus,
In the dust, under greensward—
Curse my fist! Cynfarch's son gored!

The handsome corpse is abandoned here
Under this sod, this gravestone—
Curse my fist! My liege-lord gone!

The handsome corpse is here locked away,
Made to rest beneath the rock—
Curse my fist! How the weirds knock!

The handsome corpse is settled in earth
Beneath vervain and nettle—
Curse my fist! Hear fate rattle!

The handsome corpse is laid down today,
Laid under this earth and stone—
Curse my fist! This fate was mine!

—Anonymous
Translated by Wesli Court

ENGLYN MILWR (eng'-lin meal'-oor). Welsh in origin. A rhymed triplet with seven-syllable lines.

```
sssssss        a
sssssss        a
sssssss        a
```

THE HEAD OF URIEN

I carry a severed head.
Cynfarch's son, its owner, would
Charge two warbands without heed.

I bear a great warrior's skull.
Many did good Urien rule;
On his bright breast, a grey gull.

I bear a head at my heart,
Urien's head, who ruled a court;
On his bright breast the crows dart.

I bear a head in my hand.
A shepherd in Yrechwydd-land,
Spear-breaker, kingly and grand.

I bear a head at my thigh,
Shield of the land, battle-scythe,
Column of war, falcon-cry.

I bear a head sinister.
His life great, his grave bitter,
The old warriors' savior.

I bear a head from the hills.
His hosts are lost in the vales.
Lavish it with cries and hails.

I bear a head on my shield.
I stood my ground in the field
Near at hand—he would not yield.

I bear a head on my greaves.
After battlecry he gives
Brennych's land its laden graves.

I bear a head in my hand,
Gripped hard. Well he ruled the land
In peace or in war's command.

I cut and carried this head
That kept me fearless of dread—
Sever my quick hand instead!

I bear a head from the wood,
Upon its mouth frothing blood
And, hereafter, on Rheged!

My breast quaked and my arm shook;
My heart was stone, and it broke.
I bear the head that I took.

—Anonymous

Translated by Wesli Court

DIMETER QUATRAIN. Probably American in origin, it suggests the SKELETONIC COUPLET in its rapid movement.

$\cup\,/\quad\cup\,/$ a
$\cup\,/\quad\cup\,/$ b
$\cup\,/\quad\cup\,/$ a
$\cup\,/\quad\cup\,/$ b

FOR MY CONTEMPORARIES

How time reverses
The proud in heart!
I now make verses
Who aimed at art.

But I sleep well.
Ambitious boys
Whose big lines swell
With spiritual noise,

Despise me not,
And be not queasy
To praise somewhat:
Verse is not easy.

But rage who will.
Time that procured me
Good sense and skill
Of madness cured me.
                    —J. V. Cunningham

George Garrett employs the dimeter quatrain to evoke a mood very different from Cunningham's. Note also the breaking of the pattern of rhyme in the penultimate stanza and the return to it in the last one, an effective resolving move.

TIRESIAS

Speak to us who
are also split.
Speak to the two
we love and hate.

You have been both
and you have known
the double truth
as, chaste, obscene,

you were the lover
and the loved.
You were the giver
who received.

Now tell us how
we can be one

another too.
Speak to us who

in single wrath
cannot be true
to life or death.
Blinder than you.
　　　　　—George Garrett

COMMON MEASURE. Of untraceable origin. The pattern is the same as that of the BALLAD STANZA except that the measure here is generally more firmly iambic than is the loose, conversational rhythm of the ballad, though it may be quite loose at times. The term *common measure* is used primarily to indicate that the poem built on this pattern is not a long narrative.

‿/	‿/	‿/	‿/	x
‿/	‿/	‿/		a
‿/	‿/	‿/	‿/	x
‿/	‿/	‿/		a

I HEARD A FLY BUZZ WHEN I DIED

I heard a fly buzz when I died;
　　The stillness round my form
Was like the stillness in the air
　　Between the heaves of storm.

The eyes beside had wrung them dry,
　　And breaths were gathering sure
For the last onset, when the king
　　Be witnessed in his power.

I willed my keepsakes, signed away
　　What portion of me I
Could make assignable,—and then
　　There interposed a fly,

With blue, uncertain, stumbling buzz,
　　Between the light and me;

And then the windows failed, and then
   I could not see to see.
—Emily Dickinson

HYMNAL MEASURE. Probably English in origin. A quatrain. The preferred form for hymns. Usually iambic, as shown here, but may be based on any foot. Alternately rhymed.

```
 ᵕ /    ᵕ /    ᵕ /    ᵕ /        a
 ᵕ /    ᵕ /    ᵕ /                b
 ᵕ /    ᵕ /    ᵕ /    ᵕ /        a
 ᵕ /    ᵕ /    ᵕ /                b
```

Amazing Grace, How Sweet the Sound
That Saved a wretch like me;
I once was lost, but now am found,
Was blind but now I see.
—John Newton

Hymnal measure has also been one of the most used forms for the secular poem, though it almost always suggests the hymn, directly or ironically.

A SLUMBER DID MY SPIRIT SEAL

A slumber did my spirit seal;
I had no human fears:
She seemed a thing that could not feel
The touch of earthly years.

No motion has she now, no force;
She neither hears nor sees;
Rolled round in earth's diurnal course,
With rocks, and stones, and trees.
—William Wordsworth

SHORT MEASURE. Probably English in origin. A variant of BALLAD STANZA, so-called because the first line (compared to ballad stanza) is one foot short. It appears most often in hymns. Usually iambic, but not always and not always consistently so even within the poem.

◡ /	◡ /	◡ /		x
◡ /	◡ /	◡ /		a
◡ /	◡ /	◡ /	◡ /	x
◡ /	◡ /	◡ /		a

The bustle in a house
The morning after death
Is solemnest of industries
Enacted upon earth,—

The sweeping up the heart,
And putting love away
We shall not want to use again
Until eternity.

          —Emily Dickinson

SHORT HYMNAL MEASURE. Probably English in origin. So called because it varies from HYMNAL MEASURE by the lack of one foot in the first line.

◡ /	◡ /	◡ /		a
◡ /	◡ /	◡ /		b
◡ /	◡ /	◡ /	◡ /	a
◡ /	◡ /	◡ /		b

The following poem, with the extreme slant rhyme between *moor* and *looks*, illustrates Emily Dickinson's daring way with sound.

I never saw a moor,
I never saw the sea;
Yet know I how the heather looks,
And what a billow be.

I never spoke with God,
Nor visited in heaven;

Yet certain am I of the spot
As if the checks were given.

—Emily Dickinson

LONG MEASURE. A quatrain of untraceable origin. So called because all four lines have four beats, as compared to most other quatrains, in which at least lines 2 and 4 have three stresses. Traditionally iambic. Line length and foot designation are sometimes treated rather loosely.

⌣ /	⌣ /	⌣ /	⌣ /	x
⌣ /	⌣ /	⌣ /	⌣ /	a
⌣ /	⌣ /	⌣ /	⌣ /	x
⌣ /	⌣ /	⌣ /	⌣ /	a

Here are a medieval ballad (presented in its condensed version) and a contemporary poem in long measure, which will give some sense of the adaptability of the form. Note the looser rhythm of the traditional ballad.

JOHNIE ARMSTRONG

There dwelt a man in fair Westmorland,
 Johnie Armstrong men did him call.
He had neither lands nor rents coming in,
 Yet he kept eight score men in his hall.

He had horses and harness for them all.
 Their goodly steeds were all milk-white.
O the golden bands all about their necks!
 Their weapons, they were all alike.

The news was brought unto the king
 That there was such a one as he
That lived like a bold out-law,
 And robbed all the north-countree.

The king he writ a letter then,
 A letter which was large and long,

And signed it with his own hand,
   And he promised to do him no wrong.

When this letter came to Johnie,
   His heart was as blythe as birds on the tree:
"Never was I sent for before any king,
   My father, my grandfather, nor none but me.

And if we go the king before,
   I would we went most orderly;
Let everyman wear his scarlet cloak
   Laced up with silver laces three.

Let everyman wear his velvet coat
   Laced with silver lace so white.
O the golden bands all about your necks!
   Black hats, white feathers, all alike."

By the morrow morning at ten of the clock,
   Towards Edenburough gone was he,
And with him all his eight score men.
   Good lord, it was a goodly sight to see!

When Johnie came before the king,
   He fell down on his knee.
"O pardon my sovereign liege," he said,
   "O pardon my eight score men and me!"

"Thou shalt have no pardon, thou traitor strong,
   For thy eight score men nor thee;
For tomorrow morning by ten of the clock
   Both thou and them shall hang on the gallow-tree."

But Johnie looked over his left shoulder,
   Good Lord, what a grievous look looked he!
Saying, "Asking grace of a graceless face—
   Why there is none for you nor me."

But Johnie had a bright sword by his side,
   And it was made of the mettle so free,
That had not the king stept his foot aside,
   He had smitten his head from his fair bodie.

Saying: "Fight on, my merry men all,
    And see that none of you be taine;
For rather than men shall say we were hanged,
    Let them say how we were slain."

Then, God wot, fair Edenburough rose,
    And so beset poor Johnie round,
That four score and ten of his best men
    Lay gasping all upon the ground.

Then like a mad man Johnie laid about,
    And like a mad man then fought he,
Until a false Scot come Johnie behind
    And ran him through the fair bodie.

Saying: "Fight on, my merry men all,
    And see that none of you be taine;
For I will lie down and bleed awhile,
    And then I will rise and fight again."

                        —Anonymous

VOICE OF AMERICA

Do not imagine his father lying
between his mother and falling to sleep
beside her while she wonders how
she knows, knowing she will keep

the secret for a weaker proof.
Do not imagine the million seed
moving by some myotic hunger
from dark to dark, from need to need.

Do not imagine one by luck
or fate finds the target to win
and like a bullet hitting a head
in slow motion crashes in.

Do not imagine the man starts
and terminates in the same act,
will be before the bullet stops
the zero absolute unfact

his mother remembered in reverse.
Do not imagine his father sent
the million missiles against the egg
with more joy and less intent.

Do not imagine the cells splitting.
Do not imagine the hollow ball
he was awhile, a senseless worm,
no heart, head, nothing at all,

as when his father a following day
the following month would ask "What is it?"
"It's nothing. It's honestly nothing at all."
Do not imagine the exquisite

danger when the cell divides
when a chromosome splits apart
half shifting here, half there,
to shape the kidney and the heart.

Do not imagine the enormous eyes.
Do not imagine the chin sits
soft against the uncovered heart.
Do not imagine the gill slits,

the hands unfinished, the tail shrinking.
Do not imagine the time at hand
or what it means. Raise the gun.
Hold it gently as you were trained

to hold it. Let the bullet swim
slowly into his opening head
fast as sperm   the way the films
in school can show a flower spread.

—Miller Williams

LONG HYMNAL MEASURE. A quatrain probably English in origin.
The same as LONG MEASURE, except that the rhymes are alternate, as in
HYMNAL MEASURE.

      ∪ /   ∪ /   ∪ /   ∪ /   a
      ∪ /   ∪ /   ∪ /   ∪ /   b

∪ / ∪ / ∪ / ∪ /   a
∪ / ∪ / ∪ / ∪ /   b

A LITTLE POEM

We say that some are mad. In fact
if we have all the words and we
make madness mean the way they act
then they as all of us can see

are surely mad. And then again
if they have all the words and call
madness something else, well then—
well then, they are not mad at all.

—Miller Williams

IN MEMORIAM STANZA. English in origin. A quatrain, used first (or most notably) by Tennyson for *In Memoriam*. Iambic. An "envelope stanza," *i.e.*, the "outside" lines form a rhyming pair.

∪ / ∪ / ∪ / ∪ /   a
∪ / ∪ / ∪ / ∪ /   b
∪ / ∪ / ∪ / ∪ /   b
∪ / ∪ / ∪ / ∪ /   a

Prologue to IN MEMORIAM

Strong Son of God, immortal Love,
    Whom we, that have not seen thy face,
    By faith, and faith alone, embrace,
Believing where we cannot prove;

Thine are these orbs of light and shade;
    Thou madest Life in man and brute;
    Thou madest Death; and lo, thy foot
Is on the skull which thou hast made.

Thou wilt not leave us in the dust:
    Thou madest man, he knows not why,
    He thinks he was not made to die;
And thou hast made him; thou art just.

Thou seemest human and divine,
The highest, holiest manhood, thou.
Our wills are ours, we know not how;
Our wills are ours, to make them thine.

Our little systems have their day;
They have their day and cease to be;
They are but broken lights of thee,
And thou, O Lord, art more than they.

We have but faith; we cannot know,
For knowledge is of things we see;
And yet we trust it comes from thee,
A beam in darkness; let it grow.

Let knowledge grow from more to more,
But more of reverence in us dwell;
That mind and soul, according well,
May make one music as before,

But vaster. We are fools and slight;
We mock thee when we do not fear.
But help thy foolish ones to bear;
Help thy vain worlds to bear thy light.

Forgive what seemed my sin in me,
What seemed my worth since I began;
For merit lives from man to man,
And not from man, O Lord, to thee.

Forgive my grief for one removed,
Thy creature, whom I found so fair.
I trust he lives in thee, and there
I find him worthier to be loved.

Forgive these wild and wandering cries,
Confusions of a wasted youth;
Forgive them where they fail in truth,
And in thy wisdom make me wise.

—Alfred, Lord Tennyson

ITALIAN QUATRAIN. Italian in origin; correctly named. An envelope stanza (see *IN MEMORIAM STANZA*) traditionally in iambic pentameter.

‿ /	‿ /	‿ /	‿ /	‿ /	a
‿ /	‿ /	‿ /	‿ /	‿ /	b
‿ /	‿ /	‿ /	‿ /	‿ /	b
‿ /	‿ /	‿ /	‿ /	‿ /	a

REMEMBERING WALTER

I remember when I learned he was dead.
I was halfway done with a paper route
and saw the crowd and stopped to find out
what was going on and someone said

Walter was drowned. I had to go disguised
in a borrowed boy scout uniform to take
my turn sitting beside him at the wake,
to halfway hope the skin across his eyes

would tighten against the light. I would find mud
to bless them open or find whoever knew
what it was you had to say or do.
But someone said he didn't have his blood.

What should these memories mean at forty-two?
That twelve is a highly impressionable age.
That all the rage we learn is the first rage.
That more than choose to die by water, do.

        —Miller Williams

THE COMMON WISDOM

Their marriage is a good one. In our eyes
What makes a marriage good? Well, that the tether
Fray but not break, and that they stay together.
One should be watching while the other dies.

        —Howard Nemerov

SICILIAN QUATRAIN. Sicilian in origin, often called the *heroic quatrain*, though strictly speaking all iambic pentameter quatrains are heroic. Any alternately rhymed iambic pentameter stanzas (of any length) are "Sicilian." For additional examples see EPIGRAM in the Glossary and William Meredith's "About Opera" on p. 20.

˘ /	˘ /	˘ /	˘ /	˘ /	a
˘ /	˘ /	˘ /	˘ /	˘ /	b
˘ /	˘ /	˘ /	˘ /	˘ /	a
˘ /	˘ /	˘ /	˘ /	˘ /	b

From O BROTHER MAN, FOLD TO THY HEART

O brother man, fold to thy heart thy brother!
Where pity dwells, the peace of God is there;
To worship rightly is to love each other,
Each smile a hymn, each kindly deed a prayer.

—John Greenleaf Whittier

ELEGIAC STANZA ON A PHOTOGRAPH
OF ETHEL ROSENBERG IN HER KITCHEN

It sits on top my desk, but it is faced
So that the sun will not cause it to fade:
The photographs we save are like the taste
Of honey on a sharpened razor blade.

—John A. Wood

CURTAL QUATRAIN. American in origin. Generally iambic.

˘ /	˘ /	˘ /	˘ /	˘ /	x
˘ /	˘ /	˘ /	˘ /	˘ /	a
˘ /	˘ /	˘ /	˘ /	˘ /	x
˘ /	˘ /				a

"NOT MARBLE NOR THE GILDED MONUMENTS"
for Adele

The praisers of women in their proud and beautiful poems,
Naming the grave mouth and the hair and the eyes,

Boasted those they loved should be forever remembered:
These were lies.

The words sound but the face in the Istrian sun is forgotten.
The poet speaks but to her dead ears no more.
The sleek throat is gone—and the breast that was troubled to listen:
Shadow from door.

Therefore I will not praise your knees nor your fine walking
Telling you men shall remember your name as long
As lips move or breath is spent or the iron of English
Rings from a tongue.

I shall say you were young, and your arms straight, and your mouth
    scarlet:
I shall say you will die and none will remember you:
Your arms change, and none remember the swish of your garments,
Nor the click of your shoe.

Not with my hand's strength, not with difficult labor
Springing the obstinate words to the bones of your breast
And the stubborn line to your young stride and the breath to your
    breathing
And the beat to your haste

Shall I prevail on the hearts of unborn men to remember.
(What is a dead girl but a shadowy ghost
Or a dead man's voice but a distant and vain affirmation
Like dream words most)

Therefore I will not speak of the undying glory of women.
I will say you were young and straight and your skin fair
And you stood in the door and the sun was a shadow of leaves on
    your shoulders
And a leaf on your hair—

I will not speak of the famous beauty of dead women:
I will say the shape of a leaf lay once on your hair.
Till the world ends and the eyes are out and the mouths broken
Look! It is there!

                                        —Archibald MacLeish

The limitations of a form in imposing voice, tone, and pacing become clear in a comparison of MacLeish's lines with those in the following poem.

LATE SHOW

Too tired to sleep I switch a picture on,
turn down the sound to let my attention drain.
A forest in summer. Dogs. A man is running.
It's starting to rain.

The man comes to a house. He breaks a window.
A girl getting out of the shower admiring herself
looks to see if the cat has knocked something
from the kitchen shelf.

She sees the man. She wraps a towel about her.
In the woods loosed from their leashes the dogs
are running circles scratching at empty trees
sniffing at logs.

The woman is breathing behind a chair in the kitchen.
The man is leaning against the kitchen door.
Her mouth moves. He hits her in the face.
She falls to the floor.

He tears the towel away. He stands above her.
He looks a long time. He lets her curl
into a corner. Both of us can see
she is only a girl.

He takes her to her bed and drops her in it.
Looks at her as if he has not seen her
before now. Takes off his clothes and puts
himself between her.

He moves his lips. She bends her legs and locks him in.
They move together. I turn up the sound.
They stop moving. They look in my direction.
A single hound

is crouping close. She shoves the man aside,
rolls out of bed, runs with nothing around her
into the rain, into the leaping dogs.
Lightning and thunder.

He sits on the bed, his back a slow curve.
Turn it off, he says, in god's name.
The door opens. A man with a long gun.
He takes aim.

—Miller Williams

SAPPHICS. Derived from Greek verse. An unrhymed quatrain. The first three lines are trochaic except for the central foot in each line, which is a dactyl. The fourth is a short line called an *adonic*, composed of a dactyl followed by a trochee.

/ ◡	/ ◡	/ ◡◡	/ ◡	/ ◡	x
/ ◡	/ ◡	/ ◡◡	/ ◡	/ ◡	x
/ ◡	/ ◡	/ ◡◡	/ ◡	/ ◡	x
/ ◡◡	/ ◡				x

VISITOR

Visitor, you've come and have gone while I was
gone, while winds were moving through open windows,
billowing the drapes in my vacant chambers,
  sounding the silence;

come and gone, whoever you were, and left no
note but quiet sliding among the shadows.
Here before my house, by the stolid doorway,
  I remain watching—

listening where you must have lingered, waiting
I stand listening for the bell's thin echo,
knowing for a certainty you were here and
  left without echo.

All will turn out differently now. Behind this
door there stands an alien future. Words that

needed speaking have not been spoken, and the
            time that has not been

spent correctly now must be handled strangely,
sold less truly: used in another manner.
Sounds have not been breasted. The stillness thickens
            over your footfalls.

Visitor, between us are tunnels sealed and
hollow; there are depths where once there were crossings.
There are windows, too, gone opaque with wonder,
            darkling with questions.

                                        —Lewis Turco

AWDL GYWYDD (ow̓-dull guh̓-with). Welsh in origin. A quatrain stanza in seven-syllable lines. Lines 2 and 4 rhyme; lines 1 and 3 rhyme with (or may only slightly echo) any one internal syllable of lines 2 and 4 respectively.

sssssss	a
sssssss	b
sssssss	c
sssssss	b

SPRING SONG

Earthspring, the sweetest season,
Loud the birdsong, sprouts ripple,
Plough in furrow, ox in yoke,
Sea like smoke, fields in stipple.

Yet when cuckoos call from trees
I drink the lees of sorrow;
Tongue bitter, I sleep with pain—
My kinsmen come not again.

On mountain, mead, seaborne land,
Wherever man wends his way,

What path he take boots not,
He shall not keep from Christ's eye.
—Anonymous (*ca.* Tenth century)
Translated by Wesli Court

ENGLYN PROEST DALGRON (eng'-lin proyst dahl'-grown). Welsh in origin. Quatrains of seven-syllable lines all ending in assonantal rhymes.

sssssss   *or*
sssssss   *or*
sssssss   *or*
sssssss   *or*

THE GRAVE

Everyman comes to the dank earth.
Folk, forlorn and small, perish.
What wealth rears is wracked by death.
In an hour dirt devoureth.

Great maw, end of what I clutch,
What I loved you turn to filth.
Mine will be a chill stone hearth—
Life was not meant for a youth.

Each man's cold estate is death;
He walks alone on the heath
That will take him in its clinch,
Come at last to the cromlech.
—Dafydd Benfras (Thirteenth century)
Translated by Wesli Court

CINQUAIN. Originally a five-line French stanza with any rhyme scheme or none and of uncertain line length. The American poet Adelaide Crapsey applied the term to a set form that she had devised, with unrhymed lines of two, four, six, eight, and two syllables, respectively. The lines usually scan iambic.

She likes
To walk around
On Sunday afternoons
With absolutely nothing on
Her mind.

—Clement Long

HEROIC SESTET. Probably Sicilian in origin. Traditionally iambic pentameter, with alternate rhymes followed by a rhymed couplet; *i.e.*, a SICILIAN QUATRAIN joined to a HEROIC COUPLET.

∪ /	∪ /	∪ /	∪ /	∪ /	a
∪ /	∪ /	∪ /	∪ /	∪ /	b
∪ /	∪ /	∪ /	∪ /	∪ /	a
∪ /	∪ /	∪ /	∪ /	∪ /	b
∪ /	∪ /	∪ /	∪ /	∪ /	c
∪ /	∪ /	∪ /	∪ /	∪ /	c

From THE CITY OF DREADFUL NIGHT

Because he seemed to walk with an intent
    I followed him; who, shadowlike and frail,
Unswervingly though slowly onward went,
    Regardless, wrapt in thought as in a veil:
Thus step for step with lonely sounding feet
We travelled many a long dim silent street.

At length he paused: a black mass in the gloom,
    A tower that merged into the heavy sky;
Around, the huddled stones of grave and tomb:
    Some old God's-acre now corruption's sty:
He murmured to himself with full despair,
Here Faith died, poisoned by this charnel air.

Then turning to the right went on once more,
    And travelled weary roads without suspense;
And reached at last a low wall's open door,
    Whose villa gleamed beyond the foliage dense:

He gazed, and muttered with a hard despair,
Here Love died, stabbed by its own worshipped pair.

Then turning to the right resumed his march,
    And travelled streets and lanes with wondrous strength,
Until on stooping through a narrow arch
    We stood before a squalid house at length:
He gazed, and whispered with cold despair,
Here Hope died, starved out in its utmost lair.

When he had spoken thus, before he stirred,
    I spoke, perplexed by something in the signs
Of desolation I had seen and heard
    In this drear pilgrimage to ruined shrines:
When Faith and Love and Hope are dead indeed,
Can Life still live? By what doth it proceed?

As whom his one intense thought overpowers,
    He answered coldly, Take a watch, erase
The signs and figures of the circling hours,
    Detach the hands, remove the dial-face;
The works proceed until run down; although
Bereft of purpose, void of use, still go.

Then turning to the right paced on again,
    And traversed squares and travelled streets whose glooms
Seemed more and more familiar to my ken;
    And reached that sullen temple of the tombs;
And paused to murmur with the old despair,
Here Faith died, poisoned by this charnel air.

I ceased to follow, for the knot of doubt
    Was severed sharply with a cruel knife:
He circled thus for ever tracing out
    The series of the fraction left of Life;
Perpetual recurrence in the scope
Of but three terms, dead Faith, dead Love, dead Hope.

—James Thomson

SICILIAN SESTET. Its name correctly identifies the stanza's origin. Traditionally iambic pentameter, alternately rhymed.

```
 ∪ /      ∪ /      ∪ /      ∪ /      ∪ /          a
 ∪ /      ∪ /      ∪ /      ∪ /      ∪ /          b
 ∪ /      ∪ /      ∪ /      ∪ /      ∪ /          a
 ∪ /      ∪ /      ∪ /      ∪ /      ∪ /          b
 ∪ /      ∪ /      ∪ /      ∪ /      ∪ /          a
 ∪ /      ∪ /      ∪ /      ∪ /      ∪ /          b
```

The need for two three-rhyme sets in each stanza has made the form less than popular in English, in which the HEROIC SESTET has been much preferred.

JORDAN

When first my lines of heav'nly joys made mention,
Such was their luster, they did so excel,
That I sought out quaint words and trim invention;
My thoughts began to burnish, sprout, and swell,
Curling with metaphors a plain intention,
Decking the sense as if it were to sell.

Thousands of notions in my brain did run,
Off'ring their service, if I were not sped.
I often blotted what I had begun:
This was not quick enough, and that was dead.
Nothing could seem too rich to clothe the sun,
Much less those joys which trample on his head.

As flames do work and wind when they ascend,
So did I weave myself into the sense.
But while I bustled, I might hear a friend
Whisper, "How wide is all this long pretense!
There is in love a sweetness ready penned,
Copy out only that, and save expense."

—George Herbert

SHORT SESTET. American in origin. Tripodic; iambic or anapestic.

```
 ∪ ∪ /      ∪ ∪ /      ∪ ∪ /          x
 ∪ ∪ /      ∪ ∪ /      ∪ ∪ /          a
 ∪ ∪ /      ∪ ∪ /      ∪ ∪ /          x
```

∪∪ /   ∪∪ /   ∪∪ /   a
∪∪ /   ∪∪ /   ∪∪ /   x
∪∪ /   ∪∪ /   ∪∪ /   a

THE OUTING

NEWTON, MASS., April 20: Five women ranging in age from 80 to 96 drowned this afternoon when a driverless car rolled across a rest home lawn and sank in Crystal Lake.—*The New York Times*

It was more like a dream than an ending,
the lawn chairs adrift on the grass,
the elm trees parting politely
so that ladies kept waiting might pass
before Bartlett returns from the pantry
where he's won some affection at last.

They enter the lake without Bartlett,
and settle down in the sand;
the windows are closed, except Bartlett's,
the handle comes off in the hand;
and Bartlett goes right on romancing,
knowing that they'll understand.

They sit as they sat as they waited
for Bartlett in fine livery
who's taking them all Sunday driving
and bringing them back for tea,
but Bartlett has conquered some virtue
and lingers inside wistfully.

And now though he's diving to find them,
and even holds open the door,
there is little to say of his sorrow
as he floats them each back to the shore
where the others have come to verandas
to see the five ladies once more.

                —Dan Masterson

SPLIT SESTET. American in origin. Iambic trimeter with a single anapest serving as lines 3 and 6.

```
 ∪ /      ∪ /      ∪ /              a
 ∪ /      ∪ /      ∪ /              a
∪∪ /                               b
 ∪ /      ∪ /      ∪ /              a
 ∪ /      ∪ /      ∪ /              a
∪∪ /                               b
```

THE LAST LEAF

I saw him once before,
As he passed by the door,
    And again
The pavement stones resound,
As he totters o'er the ground
    With his cane.

They say that in his prime,
Ere the pruning-knife of Time
    Cut him down,
Not a better man was found
By the Crier on his round
    Through the town.

But now he walks the streets,
And he looks at all he meets
    Sad and wan,
And he shakes his feeble head,
That it seems as if he said,
    "They are gone."

The mossy marbles rest
On the lips that he has prest
    In their bloom,
And the names he loved to hear
Have been carved for many a year
    On the tomb.

My grandmamma has said—
Poor old lady, she is dead
    Long ago—

That he had a Roman nose,
And his cheek was like a rose
    In the snow;

But now his nose is thin,
And it rests upon his chin
    Like a staff,
And a crook is in his back,
And a melancholy crack
    In his laugh.

I know it is a sin
For me to sit and grin
    At him here;
But the old three-cornered hat,
And the breeches, and all that,
    Are so queer!

And if I should live to be
The last leaf upon the tree
    In the spring,
Let them smile, as I do now,
At the old forsaken bough
    Where I cling.

              —Oliver Wendell Holmes

CLOGYRNACH (cloh-guhr′-nach). Welsh in origin. A sestet stanza with lines of eight, eight, five, five, three, and three syllables respectively. Rhymed as shown.

s s s s s s s s	a
s s s s s s s s	a
s s s s s	b
s s s s s	b
s s s	b
s s s	a

The stanza is sometimes written as a quintet with the three-syllable lines becoming a single six-syllable line.

```
s s s s s s s s        a
s s s s s s s s        a
s s s s s              b
s s s s s              b
s s s s s s            a
```

IN SUMMER

Summer I love, stallions abroad,
Knights courageous before their lord;
    The comber booming,
    Apple tree blooming,
  Shield shining, war-shouldered.

Longing, I went craving, alack—
The bowing of the slim hemlock,
    In bright noon, dawn's sleight;
    Fair frail form smooth, white,
  Her step light on the stalk.

Silent is the small deer's footfall,
Scarcely older than she is tall.
    Comely, beautiful,
    Bred bountiful,
  Passion will heed her call,

But no vile word will pass her lips.
I pace, I plead—when shall we tryst?
    When will you meet me?
    Love drowns me deeply—
  Christ keep me! He knows best.
        —Hywel ab Owain Gwynedd
          (Twelfth century)
        Translated by Wesli Court

RIME ROYAL. Probably French in origin. A seven-line stanza with ten syllables per line; in English the measure tends to become accentual-syllabic, with five iambs per line. Called *royal* because it was preferred for his own verses by James I of Scotland, who borrowed it from Chaucer. The rhyme sequence by line is ababbcc. Rime royal describes each of the longer stanzas in the following poems, not the poems themselves.

COMPLAINT TO HIS PURSE

To you, my purse, and to noon other wight,
Complaine I, for ye be my lady dere.
I am so sory, now that ye be light,
For certes, but if ye make me hevy cheere,
Me were as lief be laid upon my beere;
For which unto youre mercy thus I crye:
Beeth hevy again, or elles moot I die.

Now voucheth sauf this day ere it be night
That I of you the blisful soun may heere.
Or see youre colour, lik the sonne bright,
That of yelownesse hadde nevere peere.
Ye be my life, ye be myn hertes steere,
Queene of confort and of good compaignye:
Beeth hevy again, or elles moot I die.

Ye purse, that been to me my lives light
And saviour, as in this world down here,
Out of this tonne helpe me thurgh your might,
Sith that ye wol nat be my tresorere;
For I am shave as neigh as any frere.
But yit I praye unto youre courteisye:
Beeth hevy again, or elles moot I die.

ENVOY TO HENRY IV

O conquerour of Brutus Albioun,
Which that by line and free eleccioun
Been verray king, this song to you I sende:
And ye, that mowen alle oure harmes amende,
Have minde upon my supplicacioun.

—Geoffrey Chaucer

THOUGHTS FROM THE BOSTON POST ROAD

Today a thousand vehicles have passed
    In cussing columns down the nearby Post
Road, left that sparrow on the billboard gassed
    Whose muddled instincts panic to the west
    Beyond the screws and monkeywrenches tossed
    From mobile windows. But the west is east,
    And east is south, and south is north at least.

The land is shot for sparrows, shot for men.
    But for machines it's Paradise on Wheels.
The lubricated sky remembers when
    Its clouds were H_2O, not high grade oils;
    And everywhere the graded turf recalls
    When it grew grasses rather than these goddam
    Vines of white concrete and black macadam.

If that poor sparrow ever manages
    To climb above our gamma-powered smogs,
Let him look down upon these acreages
    And see if apple trees are bearing cogs—
    Or if some tractor isn't laying eggs,
    Its mate a diesel truck that proudly roars
    To herald a new age of dinosaurs.

We've done a grand job building road and rail.
    There's nowhere some good engine cannot roll
(With some good man behind the driver's wheel).
    And I would not be worrying at all
    Except, this afternoon, out in the hall,
    I overheard my vacuum cleaner say,
    "They built Der Furor just the other day."

                    —Lewis Turco

OTTAVA RIMA. An eight-line stanza derived from Italian poetry. Six alternately rhymed five-stress lines followed by a rhymed couplet.

ᴗ /	ᴗ /	ᴗ /	ᴗ /	ᴗ /	a
ᴗ /	ᴗ /	ᴗ /	ᴗ /	ᴗ /	b
ᴗ /	ᴗ /	ᴗ /	ᴗ /	ᴗ /	a
ᴗ /	ᴗ /	ᴗ /	ᴗ /	ᴗ /	b
ᴗ /	ᴗ /	ᴗ /	ᴗ /	ᴗ /	a
ᴗ /	ᴗ /	ᴗ /	ᴗ /	ᴗ /	b
ᴗ /	ᴗ /	ᴗ /	ᴗ /	ᴗ /	c
ᴗ /	ᴗ /	ᴗ /	ᴗ /	ᴗ /	c

From DON JUAN

Most epic poets plunge *"in medias res"*
   (Horace makes this the heroic turnpike road),
And then your hero tells, whene'er you please,
   What went before—by way of episode,
While seated after dinner at his ease,
   Beside his mistress in some soft abode,
Palace, or garden, paradise, or cavern,
Which serves the happy couple for a tavern.
        —George Gordon, Lord Byron

HANK FEDDER

Hank Fedder is my name. My wife is Maude
Fedder—she's a good woman, the neighbors
say. And she is, I guess. She's sure no bawd,
and that's God's truth. Goodness just about pours
out of her. Depends on what you call "good,"
of course. She's **good** in the house, out of doors,
at market, in her clubs—just anyplace.
Except in bed. There, she rubs my face

in the "dirt" she calls my "male mind." She makes
me sick of myself, of what I need to
do. She cuts my guts out, and then she takes
what's left of me, sets it in the window
like a dummy, calls it "Hubby," "Dad," bakes
cakes for it, and sends it off to work. Oh,
yes, she's good all right. She makes a fine spouse.
On her bridge night I come to this whorehouse

to salvage what's left of my need, of my
insides. It never works. I leave here done
to death with sickness, the sickness that I
have now, truly, just as she claims. She's won
her point. I'm not the man she married by
a long shot—no man at all. And my son,
our son . . . he knows it, hates the "hubby" of
that best of mothers he will always love.

—Lewis Turco

SPENSERIAN STANZA. English in origin. A nine-line stanza, rhymed as shown below. Named for Sir Edmund Spenser, who invented it. The first eight lines have five stresses and are traditionally iambic; the ninth line is iambic hexameter, called an *Alexandrine line*, a term applied to any terminal line in iambic hexameter.

∪ /	∪ /	∪ /	∪ /	∪ /		a
∪ /	∪ /	∪ /	∪ /	∪ /		b
∪ /	∪ /	∪ /	∪ /	∪ /		a
∪ /	∪ /	∪ /	∪ /	∪ /		b
∪ /	∪ /	∪ /	∪ /	∪ /		b
∪ /	∪ /	∪ /	∪ /	∪ /		c
∪ /	∪ /	∪ /	∪ /	∪ /		b
∪ /	∪ /	∪ /	∪ /	∪ /		c
∪ /	∪ /	∪ /	∪ /	∪ /	∪ /	c

From ADONAIS

The One remains, the many change and pass;
Heaven's light forever shines, Earth's shadows fly;
Life, like a dome of many-coloured glass,
Stains the white radiance of Eternity,
Until Death tramples it to fragments.—Die,
If thou wouldest be with that which thou dost seek!
Follow where all is fled!—Rome's azure sky,
Flowers, ruins, statues, music, words, are weak
The glory they transfuse with fitting truth to speak.

—Percy Bysshe Shelley

2 ✒ Loosely Defined Traditional Stanza Patterns

GHAZAL. The classical pattern in Arabic and Persian, in which it is rhymed. In English a series of unrhymed, sometimes loosely connected, couplets of any length, identified as couplets only because each one ends in a full or nearly full stop.

ENCOUNTER

"We," said my young radical neighbor, smashing my window,
"speak the essential conscience of mankind."

"If it comes to no more than small breakage," I said, "speak away.
But tell me, isn't smashing some fun for its own sake."

"We will not be dismissed as frivolous," he said,
grabbing my crowbar and starting to climb to the roof.

"You are seriously mistaken," I said, raising my shotgun.
"Please weigh seriously how close the range is."

"Fascist!" he said, climbing down. "Or are you a liberal
trying to fake me with no shells in that thing?"

"I'm a lamb at windows, a lion on roofs," I told him.
"You'll more or less have to guess for yourself what's loaded

until you decide to call what may be a bluff.
Meanwhile, you are also my neighbor's son:

if you'll drop that crowbar and help me pick up this glass,
I could squeeze a ham-on-rye from my tax structure,

and coffee to wash it down while we sit and talk
about my need of windows and yours to smash them."

"Not with a lumpen-liberal pseudo-fascist!"
he sneered, and jumped the fence to his own yard.

There's that about essential consciences:
given young legs, they have no trouble at fences.

—John Ciardi

TERCET (TRIPLET). Of untraceable origin. Three lines of any (but not necessarily equal) length and in any meter, with any rhyme pattern. There are almost limitless possibilities for tone and pacing.

TO A FAIR LADY, PLAYING WITH A SNAKE

Strange! that such horror and such grace
Should dwell together in one place;
A fury's arm, an angel's face!

'Tis innocence, and youth, which makes
In Chloris' fancy such mistakes,
To start at love, and play with snakes

By this and by her coldness barred,
Her servants have a task too hard;
The tyrant has a double guard!

Thrice happy snake! that in her sleeve
May boldly creep; we dare not give
Our thoughts so unconfined a leave.

Contented in that nest of snow
He lies, as he his bliss did know,
And to the wood no more would go.

Take heed, fair Eve! you do not make
Another tempter of this snake;
A marble one so warmed would speak.

—Edmund Waller

COUNTDOWN

Synchronize the falling clocks
Wind the mind and check the locks
Pick-up sticks and building blocks

pyramid to perfect knowing
minus ten and time is growing
small at nine is cold and snowing

eight is wheels and seven rain
what equation can explain
going backward in the brain
　　　　　　　　　—Miller Williams

BALLAD STANZA. Of untraceable origin. Four lines, alternately of four and three beats; sometimes with a refrain in any meter, but usually iambic, with any rhyme pattern or unrhymed. The following probably represents the most popular ballad form, if the indications of feet are taken loosely.

$$\smile / \quad \smile / \quad \smile / \quad \smile / \qquad\qquad x$$
$$\smile / \quad \smile / \quad \smile / \qquad\qquad\qquad a$$
$$\smile / \quad \smile / \quad \smile / \quad \smile / \cdot \qquad\quad x$$
$$\smile / \quad \smile / \quad \smile / \qquad\qquad\qquad a$$

Or the fourth line may be:

$$\smile / \quad \smile / \quad \smile / \quad \smile / \qquad\qquad A$$

The ballad is traditionally a narrative form used to tell a story. The anonymous ballads that are a part of our popular culture, such as "Barbara Allen," were meant to be sung. They are characterized by the omission of all but the major moments of the stories they tell—*i.e.*, of all but the most memorable moments, since in a song passed orally through many generations, only the parts most compelling to the memory would remain. This is sometimes referred to as "leaping and lingering," leaping over relatively unimportant details and lingering over the most dramatic and central parts of a story. Later and contemporary versions, called *composed* or *literary* ballads, are notable for attention to the minor actions and other details that the anonymous ballads surely included in their earliest forms.

The ballad, especially the literary ballad, in the sense of a long singable poem that tells a story (usually of love or adventure), has been written in many verse forms, but nearly always in one of the quatrains.

The third line is sometimes made to rhyme with itself:

$$\cup\ /\quad\ \cup\ /\quad\ \cup\ /\quad\ \cup\ /$$
$$\quad\ a\qquad\qquad\ a$$

Some of the stanzas of Coleridge's *The Rime of the Ancient Mariner* follow this pattern.

The difference between composed and traditional ballads in the treatment of textual details is evident in a comparison of Coleridge's poem (only the first stanzas of which are given here) with "Dives and Lazarus," an anonymous ballad out of the oral tradition.

From THE RIME OF THE ANCIENT MARINER

It is an ancient Mariner,
And he stoppeth one of three.
"By thy long grey beard and glittering eye,
Now wherefore stopp'st thou me?

The Bridegroom's doors are open'd wide,
And I am next of kin;
The guests are met, the feast is set:
May'st hear the merry din."

He holds him with his skinny hand,
"There was a ship," quoth he.
"Hold off! Unhand me, grey-beard loon!"
Eftsoons his hand dropt he.

He holds him with his glittering eye—
The Wedding-Guest stood still,
And listens like a three years' child:
The Mariner hath his will.

The Wedding-Guest sat on a stone:
He cannot choose but hear;
And thus spake on that ancient man,
The bright-eyed Mariner.

"The ship was cheer'd, the harbour clear'd,
Merrily did we drop

Below the kirk, below the hill,
Below the lighthouse top."

DIVES AND LAZARUS

As it fell out upon a day,
  Rich Dives he made a feast,
And he invited all his friends,
  And gentry of the best.

Then Lazarus laid him down and down,
  And down at Dives' door:
"Some meat, some drink, brother Dives,
  Bestow upon the poor."

"Thou art none of my brother, Lazarus,
  That lies begging at my wall:
No meat nor drink will I give thee,
  Nor bestow upon the poor."

Then Lazarus laid him down and down,
  And down at Dives' wall:
"Some meat, some drink, brother Dives,
  Or with hunger starve I shall."

"Thou art none of my brother, Lazarus,
  That lies begging at my wall:
No meat nor drink will I give thee,
  But with hunger starve you shall."

Then Lazarus laid him down and down,
  And down at Dives' gate;
"Some meat, some drink, brother Dives,
  For Jesus Christ his sake."

"Thou art none of my brother, Lazarus,
  That lies begging at my gate;
No meat nor drink will I give thee,
  For Jesus Christ his sake."

Then Dives sent out his merry men,
  To whip poor Lazarus away;

They had no power to strike a stroke,
    But flung their whips away.

Then Dives sent out his hungry dogs,
    To bite him as he lay;
They had no power to bite at all,
    But licked his sores away.

As it fell out upon a day,
    Poor Lazarus sickened and died;
Then came two angels out of heaven
    His soul therein to guide.

"Rise up, rise up, brother Lazarus,
    And go along with me;
For you've a place prepared in heaven,
    To sit on an angel's knee."

As it fell out upon a day,
    Rich Dives sickened and died;
Then came two serpents out of hell,
    His soul therein to guide.

"Rise up, rise up, brother Dives,
    And go with us to see
A dismal place, prepared in hell,
    From which thou canst not flee."

Then Dives looked up with his eyes,
    And saw poor Lazarus blest:
"Give me one drop of water, brother Lazarus,
    To quench my flaming thirst.

"Oh had I as many years to abide
    As there are blades of grass,
Then there would be an end, but now
    Hell's pains will ne'er be past.

"Oh was I now but alive again,
    The space of one half hour!
Oh that I had my peace secure!
    Then the devil should have no power."

                        —Anonymous

The ballad stanza can be put to very effective use in the short lyric, as seen in this anonymous poem, also from oral tradition.

THE UNQUIET GRAVE

"The wind doth blow today, my love,
    And a few small drops of rain;
I never had but one true-love,
    In cold grave she was lain.

"I'll do as much for my true-love
    As any young man may;
I'll sit and mourn all at her grave
    For a twelvemonth and a day."

The twelvemonth and a day being up,
    The dead began to speak:
"Oh who sits weeping on my grave,
    And will not let me sleep?"

"'Tis I, my love, sits on your grave,
    And I will not let you sleep;
For I crave one kiss of your clay-cold lips,
    And that is all I seek."

"You crave one kiss of my clay-cold lips,
    But my breath smells earthy strong;
If you have one kiss of my clay-cold lips,
    Your time will not be long.

"'Tis down in yonder garden green,
    Love, where we used to walk,
The finest flower that e'er was seen
    Is withered to a stalk.

"The stalk is withered dry, my love,
    So will our hearts decay;
So make yourself content, my love,
    Till God calls you away."

                        —Anonymous

QUINTILLA. A Spanish stanza with five eight-syllable lines (the measure tends to become iambic in English) with any of the following rhyme schemes.

a	a	a	a
b	b	b	a
a	b	a	b
b	a	a	b
a	b	b	a

From THE LOVERS OF RUBY LEE: A VERSE PLAY

Lord, I try to live as I ought.
I always go my mother's bail.
I don't rob churches, Lord. I bought
some crutches for the man I caught
watching Ruby Lee inhale.

Though I have backslid, out and in,
I tell you this, Lord, face to face,
and been where I ought not have been
I never really cared for sin.
It's just the world's a sinful place.

—Clement Long

BOB AND WHEEL. Not a stanza in itself, the bob and wheel is an appendage to a stanza, usually consisting of five lines measured in syllables, and rhymed as follows.

s s	or	s s	a
s s s s s s s		s s s s s	b
s s s s s s		s s s s s	a
s s s s s s s		s s s s s	b
s s s s s s		s s s s s	a

The short line, which in some poems is present alone, is the bob; the quatrain is the wheel. If all lines in the set are of the same length, the entire appendage is called a wheel and there is no bob. The device was popular during the Middle Ages, as evidenced in these initial stanzas from *Sir Gawain and the Green Knight*.

When the siege and assault ceased at Troy, and the city
Was broken, and burned all to brands and to ashes,
The warrior who wove there the web of his treachery
Tried was for treason, the truest on earth.
'Twas Aeneas, who later with lords of his lineage
Of well-nigh the whole of the wealth of the West Isles.
Then swiftly to Rome rich Romulus journeyed
And soon with great splendor builded that city,
Named with his own name, as now we still know it.
Ticius to Tuscany turns for his dwellings;
In Lombardy Langobard lifts up his homes;
And far o'er the French flood fortunate Brutus
With happiness Britain on hillsides full broad
   Doth found.
   War, waste, and wonder there
   Have dwelt within it bound;
   And bliss has changed to care
   In quick and shifting round.

And after this famous knight founded his Britain,
Bold lords were bred there, delighting in battle,
Who many times dealt in destruction. More marvels
Befell in those fields since the days of their finding
Than anywhere else upon earth that I know of.
Yet of all kings who came there was Arthur most comely;
My intention is, therefore, to tell an adventure
Strange and surprising, as some men consider,
A strange thing among all the marvels of Arthur.
And if you will list to the lay for a little,
Forthwith I shall tell it, as I in the town
   Heard it told
   As it doth fast endure
   In story brave and bold,
   Whose words are fixed and sure,
   Known in the land of old.

          —Anonymous
        Translated by T. H. Banks

3 ✑ Traditional Poems of Set Length*

HAIKU. An unrhymed syllabic poem, derived from Japanese verse. Lines 1 and 3 have five syllables; line 2 has seven.

```
s s s s s          x
s s s s s s s      x
s s s s s          x
```

Traditionally, there is the mention of a season of the year somewhere in a haiku, as a means of establishing the poem's tone, though this may be only the slightest suggestion.

> Uncovered, you sleep.
> Cars pass the house and I watch
> Lights on the ceiling.
> —Clement Long

CLERIHEW. English in origin. Two rhymed couplets with complex and/or comic rhymes. Any meters, lines of any lengths. Most often used for satiric purposes.

> What do you think
> Could be causing this terrible stink?
> I would say if I were to offer a conjecture
> A lecture.
> —Clement Long

RUBAIYAT. Persian in origin. A quatrain, traditionally iambic. Five-stress lines. Lines 1, 2, and 4 are rhymed.

---

*See also SKELTONIC COUPLET, p. 25.

∪ /	∪ /	∪ /	∪ /	∪ /	a
∪ /	∪ /	∪ /	∪ /	∪ /	a
∪ /	∪ /	∪ /	∪ /	∪ /	x
∪ /	∪ /	∪ /	∪ /	∪ /	a

Popularized in English by Edward FitzGerald's inventive translation of the rubaiyat stanzas of the Persian poet Omar Khayyám, which as a body of work established the verse as contemplative to the point of melancholy. The following quatrain is Verse XIII of the collection. (See also p. 19.)

> Some for the Glories of This World; and some
> Sigh for the Prophet's Paradise to come;
> Ah, take the Cash, and let the Credit go,
> Nor heed the rumble of a distant Drum!

Robert Frost's "Stopping by Woods on a Snowy Evening" is an *interlocking rubaiyat, i.e.,* rhymed aaba, bbab, ccbc, ddcd, etc.

TANKA. The tanka, like the HAIKU, is borrowed from Japanese poetry. Forms borrowed from French, a nonaccentual language, are generally adapted by English-language poets to accentual syllabics or accentuals; forms borrowed from the nonaccentual Japanese, however, have not been adapted in this way. They remain syllabic in their measures. The tanka is a five-line poem, of five, seven, five, seven, and seven syllables, respectively. The first three lines are expected to make a complete statement on which the last two comment; it is in effect, then, a HAIKU followed by an unrhymed, related couplet of fourteen syllables.

> Suddenly something
> tells me to run up a hill
> and look at the sea.
> A ship almost out of sight
> about to fall off the edge.
> —Kim, So-Wol
> Translated by Miller Williams

LIMERICK. The limerick may be the only traditional form in English not borrowed from the poetry of another language. Although the oldest known examples are in French, the name is from Limerick, Ireland. John Ciardi suggests that the Irish Brigade, which served in France for most of the eighteenth century, might have taken the form to France or developed an English version of a French form. In either case the pattern is now wedded to the place. It is a five-line poem in which lines 1, 2, and 5 are anapestic trimeters and lines 3 and 4 are anapestic dimeters, rhymed as shown.

ᵕᵕ /	ᵕᵕ /	ᵕᵕ /	a
ᵕᵕ /	ᵕᵕ /	ᵕᵕ /	a
ᵕᵕ /	ᵕᵕ /		b
ᵕᵕ /	ᵕᵕ /		b
ᵕᵕ /	ᵕᵕ /	ᵕᵕ /	a

It was first popularized by Edward Lear, who usually repeated the first line as the last (a practice now abandoned) and ended the first line with a geographical place name (a practice still generally observed).

> As I was going to Bonner,
> Upon my word of honor,
> I met a pig
> Without a wig,
> As I was going to Bonner.
> —Edward Lear

The contemporary limerick usually depends on a pun or some other turn of wit. It is also likely to be somewhat suggestive or downright dirty. The two most passionate limericists of our time are John Ciardi and Isaac Asimov, but only one limerick of Ciardi's can be printed here, and none of Asimov's.

> It took me some time to agree
> To appear in a film about me
> And my various ex-wives

Detailing our sex lives,
But I did—and they rated it G.

—John Ciardi

An amorous M.A.
Said of Cupid, the C.D.,
    "From their prodigal use,
    He is, I deduce,
The John Jacob A.H."

—Anonymous

A lady from way down in Ga.
Became quite a notable fa.
    But she faded from view
    With a quaint I.O.U.
When she signed it, "Miss Lucrezia Ba."

—Anonymous

RONDELET. French in origin. A seven-line, syllabic poem, though the measure (as always with syllabics) tends to become iambic in English. The syllable counts per line are four, eight, four, eight, eight, eight, and four. Line 1 is repeated as lines 3 and 7; the rhyme pattern interlocks between the refrain and the longer lines, as shown.

I never meant	A
for you to go. The thing you heard	b
I never meant	A
for you to hear. The night you went	a
away I knew our whole absurd	b
sweet world had fallen with a word	b
I never meant.	A

—Anonymous

The rondelet is a member of what is sometimes called the *rondeau family* of forms, a group of variations on a basic pattern that includes also the TRIOLET (the oldest of the group), the ROUNDEL, and the RONDEAU itself.

TRIOLET. French in origin. An eight-line poem dating from the thirteenth century. Once built on a ten-syllable line, the modern triolet is written in any measure with lines of any length, except that rhyming lines are of the same length. Line 1 is repeated as lines 4 and 7; line 2 is repeated as line 8. Rhymes are as shown in the first example. In addition to the two examples below, see Robert Bridges' "Triolet" on p. 15. (See also the final note on the RONDELET.)

A KISS

Rose kissed me to-day	A
Will she kiss me to-morrow	B
Let it be as it may.	a
Rose kissed me to-day.	A
But the pleasure gives way	a
To a savour of sorrow;—	b
Rose kissed me to-day,—	A
Will she kiss me to-morrow?	B

—Austin Dobson

TO A FAT LADY SEEN FROM THE TRAIN

O why do you walk through the fields in gloves,
   Missing so much and so much?
O fat white woman whom nobody loves,
Why do you walk through the fields in gloves,
When the grass is soft as the breast of doves
   And shivering sweet to the touch?
O why do you walk through the fields in gloves,
   Missing so much and so much?

—Frances Cornford

DOUBLE DACTYL. British/American in origin. Two dactylic dimeter quatrains of light verse with rhymed last lines, on which the two unaccented last syllables are missing. The first line is always "Higgledy-piggledy" and the second is a proper name. Popularized by Anthony Hecht and John Hollander.

```
/ ᴗᴗ    / ᴗᴗ         x
/ ᴗᴗ    / ᴗᴗ         x
/ ᴗᴗ    / ᴗᴗ         x
/ ᴗᴗ    /            a

/ ᴗᴗ    / ᴗᴗ         x
/ ᴗᴗ    / ᴗᴗ         x
/ ᴗᴗ    / ᴗᴗ         x
/ ᴗᴗ    /            a
```

Higgledy-piggledy
Thomas A. Edison
Dreamed up the phono as
Well as the light

Thanks to his genius e-
Lectromechanical
We can read labels of
Records at night.
                    —Anthony Harrington

Higgledy-piggledy
Euclid Geometer
Pained by the asking of
"What is the use

Studying doctrines so
Axiomatical?"
Answered acutely, "Oh,
Don't be obtuse!"
                    —Anthony Harrington

ROUNDEL. English in origin. An eleven-line poem in three stanzas of four, three, and four traditionally accentual-syllabic lines of any length, though the length of the lines (except for the repeated phrase) must be equal. The first phrase (in rare cases, the first word) of the first line is repeated as lines 4 and 11. The rhymes are as shown in the example. (See also the final note on the RONDELET.)

THE ROUNDEL

A Roundel is wrought as a ring or a starbright sphere,   B ——— a
With craft of delight and with cunning of sound
   unsought,   b
That the heart of the hearer may smile if to pleasure his
   ear   a
           A roundel is wrought.   B

Its jewel of music is carven of all or of aught—   b
Love, laughter, or mourning—remembrance of rapture
   or fear—   a
That fancy may fashion to hang in the ear of thought.   b

As a bird's quick song runs round, and the hearts in us
   hear—   a
Pause answers to pause, and again the same strain caught,   b
So moves the device whence, round as a pearl or tear,   a
       A roundel is wrought.   B

—Algernon Charles Swinburne

CURTAL SONNET. English in origin; devised by Gerard Manley Hopkins. Literally, a bobtail SONNET, but in fact its relationship to the sonnet form is more complex than that phrase suggests, as the two sonnet strophes of eight and six lines each become shortened, to six and four and a fraction. Traditionally iambic pentameter.

∪ /	∪ /	∪ /	∪ /	∪ /	a
∪ /	∪ /	∪ /	∪ /	∪ /	b
∪ /	∪ /	∪ /	∪ /	∪ /	c
∪ /	∪ /	∪ /	∪ /	∪ /	a
∪ /	∪ /	∪ /	∪ /	∪ /	b
∪ /	∪ /	∪ /	∪ /	∪ /	c
∪ /	∪ /	∪ /	∪ /	∪ /	d
∪ /	∪ /	∪ /	∪ /	∪ /	b
∪ /	∪ /	∪ /	∪ /	∪ /	c
∪ /	∪ /	∪ /	∪ /	∪ /	d
∪ /					c

PIED BEAUTY

Glory be to God for dappled things—
   For skies of couple-color as a brinded cow;
     For rose-moles all in stipple upon trout that swim;
Fresh-firecoal chestnut-falls; finches' wings;
   Landscape plotted and pieced—fold, faliow, and plough;
     And áll trádes, their gear and tackle and trim.

All things counter, original, spare, strange;
   Whatever is fickle, freckled (who knows how?)
     With swift, slow; sweet, sour; adazzle, dim;
He fathers-forth whose beauty is past change:
         Praise him.

           —Gerard Manley Hopkins

TO HIS BOOK

Wafer; thin and hard and bitter pill I
   Take from time to time; pillow I have lain
     Too long on; holding the brief dreams, the styled
Dreams, the nightmares, shadows, red flames high
   High up on mountains; wilted zinnias, rain
     On dust, and great weight, the dead dog and wild
Onions; mastodonic woman who knows how,—
   I'm tired of you, tired of your insane
     Acid eating in the brain. Sharp stones, piled
Particularly, I let you go. Sink, or float, or fly now,
         Bad child.

           —Leon Stokesbury

SHORT RONDEL. French in origin. A twelve-line poem in two six-line stanzas; syllabic, though in English the line tends to become iambic. The final line of each stanza is a repetition of the first phase in line 1. Lines are of any length, but except for the repeated phrase the lengths are uniform. Rhymes are as shown in the example. (See also the final note on the RONDELET.)

RONDEL

Kissing her hair I sat against her feet,	A ——— b
Wove and unwove it, wound and found it sweet;	b
Made fast therewith her hands, drew down her eyes,	c
Deep as deep flowers and dreamy like dim skies;	c
With her own tresses bound and found her fair,	a
Kissing her hair.	A
Sleep were no sweeter than her face to me,	d
Sleep of cold sea-bloom under the cold sea;	d
What pain could get between my face and hers?	e
What new sweet thing would love not relish worse?	e
Unless, perhaps, white death had kissed me there,	a
Kissing her hair?	A

—Algernon Charles Swinburne

RONDEAU PRIME. French in origin. A twelve-line poem divided into two stanzas of seven and five lines. Still generally syllabic, as in the French, though in English the syllabic line tends to be iambic. The opening phrase of line 1 is repeated as lines 7 and 12. Lines are of any length, but (except for the repeated phrase) equal. Rhymed as shown in the example. (See also the final note on the RONDELET.)

FOR LINDA

New gifts, old pleasures, little girl in bed,	A ——— b
cross-legged lady yawning toward your toes,	c
groping toward the bedpost, toward your clothes,	c
have they told you that your dolls are dead?	b
Hair flies wildly when you shake your head	b
free of sleep. Your bright body knows	c
new gifts, old pleasures.	A
They're only shapes, the clowns upon the spread,	b
the rabbits on the wall, when a girl goes	c
and won't come back again. But I suppose	c
you'll barely miss them, now you have instead	b
new gifts, old pleasures.	A

—Clement Long

RONDEL. French in origin. A thirteen-line poem in three stanzas of four, four, and five lines. Traditionally syllabic in English, as in the French, though in English the measure tends to become iambic. Lines are of any (but equal) length. Line 1 is repeated as lines 7 and 13; line 2 is repeated as line 8. Rhymes are as shown in the example. (See also the final note on the RONDOLET.)

A PIPER'S TUNE

The old grey piper spurs his song	A
Along the ridge I used to walk.	B
From his lapel a spiral clock	b
Dangles time to what is sung.	a
Wheezing rhythms from a lung	a
Dry as last September's chalk,	b
The old grey piper spurs his song	A
Along the ridge I used to walk.	B
Fall tolls token of the wrong	a
Winter does to those who stalk	b
August's green and preening cock.	b
For on that ridge I prowled along	a
The old grey piper spurs his song.	A

—Lewis Turco

RONDEL PRIME. French in origin. This is a RONDEL with an added fourteenth line, generally syllabic in English as in the French, though in English the measure tends to become iambic. Lines are of any (but equal) length. Line 1 is repeated as lines 7 and 13; line 2 is repeated as lines 8 and 14. Rhymes are as shown in the example. (See also the final note on the RONDOLET.)

TO A BLANK SHEET OF PAPER

Paper, inviolate, white,	A
Shall it be joy or pain?	B
Shall I of fate complain,	b
Or shall I laugh tonight?	a
Shall it be hopes that are bright?	a
Shall it be hopes that are vain?	b

| Paper, inviolate, white, | A |
| Shall it be joy or pain? | B |

A dear little hand so light,	a
A moment in mine hath lain;	b
Kind was its pressure again—	b
Ah, but it was so slight!	a

| Paper, inviolate, white, | A |
| Shall it be joy or pain? | B |

—Cosmo Monkhouse

SONNET. To the Elizabethan, the word *sonnet* meant simply "a little song" and described any short lyric poem. Thanks primarily to the influence of the Italians, it soon carried a remarkably precise meaning: a fourteen-line poem composed of eight- and six-line stanzas, each having clearly defined rhetorical roles. Stanza 1 (the *octave*) presents a situation or a problem that stanza 2 (the *sestet*) comments on or resolves. The meter in English is traditionally iambic pentameter, and the tradition is a strong one.

The two major fixed forms used in English are the Italian sonnet and the English sonnet. The Spenserian sonnet, named for Edmund Spenser, its inventor, might properly be classed as a nonce variation on the sonnet, since few poets have used it and it has not entered into the tradition. Students of poetry think of it as an established form, however, so it will be described here.

ITALIAN SONNET. Developed by the fourteenth-century Italian poet Petrarch and often called the *Petrarchan sonnet*. The rhyme scheme for the octave is abba abba. The rhyme scheme for the sestet can be either cdecde or cdcdcd. The first eight lines are called the *Italian octave*. The first option for the second stanza is called the *Italian sestet*; the second, the *Sicilian sestet*.

JUSTUS QUIDEM TU ES, DOMINE, SI DISPUTEM TECUM: VERUNTAMEN
JUSTA LOQUAR AD TE: QUARE VIA IMPIORUM PROSPERATUR? ETC.

Thou art indeed just, Lord, if I contend
With thee; but, sir, so what I plead is just.

Why do sinners' ways prosper? and why must
Disappointment all I endeavour end?
   Wert thou my enemy, O thou my friend,
How wouldst thou worse, I wonder, than thou dost
Defeat, thwart me? Oh, the sots and thralls of lust
Do in spare hours more thrive than I that spend,
Sir, life upon thy cause. See, banks and brakes
Now, leaved how thick! laced they are again
With fretty chervil, look, and fresh wind shakes
Them; birds build—but not I build; no, but strain,
Time's eunuch, and not breed one work that wakes.
Mine, O thou lord of life, send my roots rain.

                —Gerard Manley Hopkins

SPENSERIAN SONNET. A sonnet variation developed in the sixteenth century by Edmund Spenser, barely suggesting his SPEN-
SERIAN STANZA; actually, a linked series of SICILIAN QUATRAINS plus a
HEROIC COUPLET. Iambic pentameter. Rhymes are as shown in the
example.

SONNET LXXV

One day I wrote her name upon the strand,	a
But came the waves and washed it away;	b
Again I wrote it with a second hand,	a
But came the tide and made my pains his prey.	b
"Vain man," said she, "that dost in vain assay	b
A mortal thing so to immortalize,	c
For I myself shall like to this decay,	b
And eke my name be wiped out likewise."	c
"Not so" quod I, "let baser things devise	c
To die in dust, but you shall live by fame;	d
My verse your virtues rare shall eternize	c
And in the heavens write your glorious name,	d
Where, whenas death shall all the world subdue,	e
Our love shall live, and later life renew."	e

                —Edmund Spenser

ENGLISH SONNET. Developed by Shakespeare to accommodate the Italian sonnet to relatively rhyme-poor English, avoiding the requirement for triple rhymes in the sestet. The pattern is built of three SICILIAN QUATRAINS and a HEROIC COUPLET. The rhetorical pattern of the poem changes slightly with the prosodic pattern, as the terminal situation or problem presented in the octave is now dealt with tentatively in the next four lines and summarily in the terminal couplet. Some English sonnets will develop through a series of three examples in three quatrains with a conclusion in the couplet. Rhymes are as shown in the first example.

WE FILED OUR TEETH ON TROUBLE

An injun hatchet nearly split my hide	a
The spring Cub Creek muddied our cabin wall.	b
My Agnes coughed so hard she almost died.	a
Hell, we limped through summer, then fall	b
Lightnin' set the prairie running wild	c
Before a man could get a bucket out.	d
Well, we're still here and cussin'. We filed	c
Our teeth on trouble. We know what it's about.	d
Right out back we fired bricks for a school,	e
Me and Tom. I guess we would again.	f
But now some goddamn politicking fool	e
Says Dan Freeman ain't American.	f
Did we chew locusts, drink dust from a sieve,	g
So a preacher's daughter could teach us how to live?	g

—Dan Jaffe

The following poem is a strict Shakespearean sonnet; the broken fifth line somewhat disguises that fact but does not change it.

THE TRAVELLING PICKER'S PRAYER AND DREAM

Lord, forgive our drinking. Forgive our dreams
Of decency we can't shake off. Sisters
Are involved, and mothers, say our screams
That wake the whole bus up, and ministers
We come from haven't helped.

The poor are moral
But none of us have rotten teeth. Our teeth
Are good, washed by salt water. Fancy coral
Grows and forms what's called a barrier reef—
But what we're up against we can't be sure

Unless it is the sea, and the sea's too big
To drink to, and the sea's also impure
As Eve's mouth on the apple or Adam's fig.
Lord, a picker's dreams should not be cursed.
Remember the souls in the last hard town we blessed.

—James Whitehead

An interesting contrast is created here between the conversational quality instilled by the consistent enjambment of the lines (and by the diction) and the ritual effect of the sonnet form itself.

Here is the English sonnet in the hands of its inventor.

SONNET XXIX

When, in disgrace with fortune and men's eyes,
I all alone beweep my outcast state,
And trouble deaf heaven with my bootless cries,
And look upon myself and curse my fate,
Wishing me like to one more rich in hope,
Featur'd like him, like him with friends possess'd,
Desiring this man's art and that man's scope,
With what I most enjoy contented least;
Yet in these thoughts myself almost despising,
Haply I think on thee, and then my state,
Like to the lark at break of day arising
From sullen earth, sings hymns at heaven's gate;
    For thy sweet love remember'd such wealth brings
    That then I scorn to change my state with kings.

—William Shakespeare

RONDEAU. French in origin. A fifteen-line poem in which the syllabic tradition is generally followed in English (though the measure tends to become iambic). The poem is divided into three stanzas of

five, four, and six lines. The opening phrase of the first line becomes
a refrain, repeated as lines 9 and 15. Lines may be of any length,
though, except for the repeated lines, their length must be equal.
Rhymes are as shown in the first example. (See also the final note
on the RONDOLET.) The second example is a rondeau in the contemporary idiom. For a shortened form of the rondeau, see Leigh Hunt's
"Rondeau," p. 162.

WHAT IS TO COME

What is to come we know not. But we know	A ——— b
That what has been was good—was good to show,	b
Better to hide, and best of all to bear.	c
We are the masters of the days that were;	c
We have lived, we have loved, we have suffered . . .	
even so.	b
Shall we not take the ebb who had the flow?	b
Life was our friend. Now, if it be our foe—	b
Dear, though it spoil and break us!—need we care	c
What is to come?	A
Let the great winds their worst and wildest blow,	b
Or the gold weather round us mellow slow;	b
We have fulfilled ourselves, and we can dare	c
And we can conquer, though we may not share	c
In the rich quiet of the afterglow	b
What is to come.	A

—William Ernest Henley

THE BATTLE: AN INDIAN LEGEND

We gather on the rim of the canyon every year
To watch the famous battle of the war
Our ancestors fought and lost. We come to mourn
And remember those who fell. We cannot warn
The braves—we watch them fall before the spear:

This is how we teach our young the lore
Of loss and life. The phantoms raise their bare

Arms against the stranger in the walls of stone.
We gather on the rim

And see them, as through water cold and clear,
Rise and fall in dust before the stranger.
"This is what was and will ever be. Learn
From this," we tell the young, and they are torn
From child to manhood, from yearning and from fear.
We gather on the rim.

—Wesli Court

VILLANELLE. A poem of nineteen lines, originally syllabic as a French form but in English construed as iambic pentameter. The pattern is broken into five triplets and a quatrain. Line 1 is repeated as lines 6, 12, and 18; line 3 is repeated as lines 9, 15, and 19. The whole poem moves on only two rhymes, as shown in the example; the refrain lines are represented as A_1 and A_2 because they are rhyming lines.

MINUET FOR ARMY BOOTS AND ORCHESTRA

Whose tongues are twisted and whose hearts are shrunk	A_1
may play as puppets, may in that disguise	b
while towns burn in their brains, drink to be drunk.	A_2
So when God comes to catch this crumbling chunk	a
of dirt, what do we say? That we despise	b
whose tongues are twisted and whose hearts are shrunk?	A_1
If Thomas had told us the gnawed body stunk,	a
what would it change? Men knowing what men devise	b
while towns burn in their brains, drink to be drunk.	A_2
If Calvin came to tell us Christ is bunk,	a
what could he hope to teach us? Pain? Surprise?	b
Whose tongues are twisted and whose hearts are shrunk?	A_1
So the viking sails for home and is sunk,	a
so Napoleon is poisoned, so Lorca dies,	b
while towns burn in their brains. Drink to be drunk	A_2

until they lay us to sleep and slam the trunk,	a
two people more who open and close their eyes,	b
whose tongues are twisted and whose hearts are shrunk,	A_1
while towns burn in their brains. Drink to be drunk.	A_2

—Miller Williams

Donald Justice softens the form slightly by varying line lengths and surprising the reader with small variations in the repeated lines. Such shifts from an established pattern heighten the sense of immediacy and credibility as they move diction closer to conversation. When they occur in the closing lines of a poem, they also enhance the sense of resolution.

IN MEMORY OF THE UNKNOWN POET ROBERT BOARDMAN VAUGHN

But the essential advantage for a poet is not, to have a beautiful world with which to deal: it is to be able to see beneath both beauty and ugliness; to see the boredom, and the horror, and the glory.—T. S. Eliot

It was his story. It had always been his story.
It followed him, it overtook him finally—
The boredom, and the horror, and the glory.

Probably at the end he was not yet sorry,
Even as the boots were brutalizing him in the alley.
It was his story. It had always been his story,

Blown on a blue horn, full of sound and fury,
But signifying, O signifying magnificently
The boredom, and the horror, and the glory.

I picture the snow as falling without hurry
To cover the cobbles and toppled ashcans completely.
It was his story. It had always been his story.

Lately he had wandered between St. Mark's Place and the Bowery,
Already half a spirit, mumbling and muttering sadly.
O the boredom, and the horror, and the glory!

All done now. But I remember the fiery,
Hypnotic eye and the raised voice blazing with poetry.
It was his story and had always been his story—
The boredom, and the horror, and the glory.

—Donald Justice

TERZANELLE. French in origin, originally syllabic with lines of any (but equal) length. A nineteen-line poem, of five triplets and one quatrain, akin to both TERZA RIMA and the VILLANELLE. Lines 1 and 3 are repeated as lines 17 and 19 or 18 and 19, depending upon the resolution chosen by the poet. The middle line of each triplet reappears as the final line of the following triplet except in the case of the final triplet (the penultimate stanza), after which its middle line appears as the third or first line of the final quatrain, depending on the form of the resolution. The rhyme pattern is as follows.

A_1
B
A_2

b
C
B

c
D
C

d
E
D

e
F
E

f		f
A_1	or	F
F		A_1
A_2		A_2

THUNDERWEATHER

This is the moment when shadows gather
under the elms, the cornices and eaves.
This is the center of thunderweather.
The birds are quiet among these white leaves
where wind stutters, starts, then moves steadily

under the elms, the cornices, and eaves—
these are our voices speaking guardedly
about the sky, of the sheets of lightning
where wind stutters, starts, then moves steadily
into our lungs, across our lips, tightening
our throats. Our eyes are speaking in the dark
about the sky, of the sheets of lightning
that illuminate moments. In the stark
shades we inhabit, there are no words for
our throats. Our eyes are speaking in the dark
of things we cannot say, cannot ignore.
This is the moment when shadows gather,
shades we inhabit. There are no words, for
this is the center of thunderweather.

—Lewis Turco

CAUDATE SONNET. Italian in origin, developed by Francesco Berni in the sixteenth century. "A sonnet with a tail," usually composed of the Italian SONNET plus two shortened lines and two HEROIC COUP-LETS, and arranged as shown, though other "tails" in other sonnet forms are sometimes seen. It is thus twenty lines in length. The poem may be broken into its two strophes at any point near the center. The rhetorical pattern of the sonnet is rigidly observed. Here is the most popular pattern.

◡ /	◡ /	◡ /	◡ /	◡ /	a
◡ /	◡ /	◡ /	◡ /	◡ /	b
◡ /	◡ /	◡ /	◡ /	◡ /	b
◡ /	◡ /	◡ /	◡ /	◡ /	a
◡ /	◡ /	◡ /	◡ /	◡ /	a
◡ /	◡ /	◡ /	◡ /	◡ /	b
◡ /	◡ /	◡ /	◡ /	◡ /	b
◡ /	◡ /	◡ /	◡ /	◡ /	a
◡ /	◡ /	◡ /	◡ /	◡ /	c
◡ /	◡ /	◡ /	◡ /	◡ /	d
◡ /	◡ /	◡ /	◡ /	◡ /	e
◡ /	◡ /	◡ /	◡ /	◡ /	c
◡ /	◡ /	◡ /	◡ /	◡ /	d

˘ /   ˘ /   ˘ /   ˘ /   ˘ /   e

˘ /   ˘ /   ˘ /   e

˘ /   ˘ /   ˘ /   ˘ /   ˘ /   f

˘ /   ˘ /   ˘ /   ˘ /   ˘ /   f

˘ /   ˘ /   ˘ /   f

˘ /   ˘ /   ˘ /   ˘ /   ˘ /   g

˘ /   ˘ /   ˘ /   ˘ /   ˘ /   g

HIS SLIGHTLY LONGER STORY SONG

She was older, say, thirty-five or so,
And I was eighteen, maybe. She was dark
And musical, I thought, out of a book
I hadn't read, Louisiana slow,
A chance to get my ass shot off or grow
Up quickly, outdistancing the nervous pack
Of boys I ran with. I was green but trick
By trick she taught where innocence could go
When what I wanted happened. Innocence
Or ignorance? Or neither one? Or both?
She claimed she'd taken sweetness from my life.

She cried, imagining the pretty wife
I'd hammer with some grief. She said the breath
Of love—this kind—was mostly arrogance.
She'd drink and then she'd dance
Alone and naked to the radio.
She said I was her baby. I said no.
She said in time I'd throw
Away her memory. I knew she lied.
I said I loved her body, loved her pride.

—James Whitehead

RONDEAU REDOUBLÉ. French in origin. A twenty-five line poem divided into five quatrains and a quintet. Each line of the first quatrain becomes a refrain, and the first phrase of the first line is repeated as a short closing line. The lines are of any length (but, except for the final one, must be equal in length) and are generally syllabic, as in the French, though in English the measure tends to become iambic. The rhyme pattern is as shown in the example. (See also the final note on the RONDOLET.)

RONDEAU REDOUBLÉ

My soul is sick of nightingale and rose,	A ——— B_1
The perfume and the darkness of the grove;	C_1
I weary of the fevers and the throes,	B_2
And all the enervating dreams of love.	C_2
At morn I love to hear the lark, and rove	c
The meadows, where the simple daisy shows	b
Her guiltless bosom to the skies above—	c
My soul is sick of nightingale and rose.	B_1
The afternoon is sweet, and sweet repose,	b
But let me lie where breeze-blown branches move.	c
I hate the stillness where the sunbeams doze,	b
The perfume and the darkness of the grove.	C_1
I love to hear at eve the gentle dove	c
Contented coo the day's delightful close.	b
She sings of love and all the calm thereof.—	c
I weary of the fevers and the throes.	B_2
I love the night, who like a mother throws	b
Her arms round hearts that throbbed and limbs that	
strove,	c
As kind as Death, that puts an end to woes	b
And all the enervating dreams of love.	C_2
Because my soul is sick of fancies wove	c
Of fervid ecstasies and crimson glows;	b
Because the taste of cinnamon and clove	c
Palls on my palate—let no man suppose	b
My soul is sick.	A

—Cosmo Monkhouse

BALLADE. French in origin. A twenty-eight-line poem divided into three octaves and a quatrain called the *envoy* (see Glossary). The last line of each of the four stanzas is a refrain. Still generally written in syllabics, as in the French, though the syllabic line in English tends to become iambic. The lines are of any (but equal) length. The rhymes are as shown, with no rhyme word being repeated throughout the poem.

STANZAS 1, 2, and 3

a
b
a
b   ENVOY
b   b
c   c
b   b
C   C

BALLADE OF DEAD ACTORS

Where are the passions they essayed,
And where are the tears they made to flow?
Where the wild humors they portrayed
For laughing worlds to see and know?
Othello's wrath and Juliet's woe?
Sir Peter's whims and Timon's gall?
And Millamant and Romeo?
Into the night go one and all.

Where are the braveries, fresh or frayed?
The plumes, the armors—friend and foe?
The cloth of gold, the rare brocade,
The mantles glittering to and fro?
The pomp, the pride, the royal show?
The cries of war and festival?
The youth, the grace, the charm, the glow?
Into the night go one and all.

The curtain falls, the play is played:
The Beggar packs beside the Beau;
The Monarch troops, and troops the Maid;
The Thunder huddles with the Snow.

Where are the revelers high and low?
The clashing swords? The lover's call?
The dangers gleaming row on row?
Into the night go one and all.

ENVOY

Prince, in one common overthrow
The Hero tumbles with the Thrall;
As dust that drives, as straws that blow,
Into the night go one and all.

—William Ernest Henley

BALLADE WITH DOUBLE REFRAIN. French in origin. A twenty-eight-line poem divided into three octaves and a quatrain or envoy. Lines 4 and 8 of stanza 1 are repeated as the corresponding lines in stanzas 2 and 3 and as lines 2 and 4 of the envoy. Lines are of any (but equal) length and syllabic, though in English the measure tends to become iambic.

STANZAS 1, 2, and 3

a
b
a
B   ENVOY
b   b
c   B
b   c
C   C

THE BALLADE OF PROSE AND RHYME

When the roads are heavy with mire and rut,
    In November fogs, in December snows,
When the North Wind howls, and the doors are shut,
    There is place and enough for the pains of prose;—
    But whenever a scent from the whitethorn blows,
And the jasmine-stars to the casement climb,

And a Rosalind-face at the lattice shows,
Then hey!—for the ripple of laughing rhyme!

When the brain gets dry as an empty nut,
   When the reason stands on its squarest toes,
When the mind (like a beard) has a "formal cut,"
     There is place and enough for the pains of prose;—
     But whenever the May-blood stirs and glows,
And the young year draws to the "golden prime,"—
   And Sir Romeo sticks in his ears a rose,
Then hey!—for the ripple of laughing rhyme!

In a theme where the thoughts have a pedant strut,
   In a changing quarrel of "Ayes" and "Noes,"
In a starched procession of "If" and "But,"
     There is place and enough for the pains of prose;—
     But whenever a soft glance softer glows,
And the light hours dance to the trysting-time,
   And the secret is told "that no one knows,"
Then hey!—for the ripple of laughing rhyme!

ENVOY

In a work-a-day world,—for its needs and woes,
There is place and enough for the pains of prose;
But whenever the May-bells clash and chime, . . .
Then hey!—for the ripple of laughing rhyme!

                                 —Austin Dobson

SESTINA. Originally a syllabic form, now often written in iambic pentameter in English, though the lines may be of any (equal) length. The sestina is a thirty-nine-line poem, divided into six stanzas of six lines each and a terminal envoy, or *tornada*, of three lines. The same six words end the lines of each sestet, rotating their order according to a strictly prescribed pattern. The triplet contains all six words, three at the ends of the lines and three buried in the lines; some degree of latitude is traditionally allowed here.

    The invention of the sestina is generally credited to Anault Daniel, a poet and mathematician who died probably in 1210 at about the age of thirty. The form was popular with the troubadours of Provence and was adopted quickly by the Italian poets of the time, notably Petrarch and Dante. The challenge of the sestina has been enduringly attractive; probably no other pattern appears so regularly in the work of contemporary poets.

In the pattern shown, each end word is represented by a number; the words shift in order through the sestets in the sequence indicated.

STANZA 1	STANZA 2	STANZA 3	STANZA 4	STANZA 5	STANZA 6	STANZA 7
1	6	3	5	4	2	2 ——— 5
2	1	6	3	5	4	4 ——— 3
3	5	4	2	1	6	6 ——— 1
4	2	1	6	3	5	
5	4	2	1	6	3	
6	3	5	4	2	1	

The order of words in the triplet is frequently

6 ——— 5
2 ——— 4
3 ——— 1

or, especially in the contemporary sestina, some other order.

Ideally, the end words of a sestina form a natural rhetorical set, revolving about a common idea. In some, five words suggest as many aspects of the theme while the sixth manages to embody all of them or sum up the sense they create. In the first of the following examples, for instance, *rose, love, heart, sang, rhyme,* and *woe* almost tell a story, with the final word telling us what the others all add up to. Older sestinas often were printed with their repeated words italicized.

SESTINA

In fair Provence, the land of lute and *rose,*
Arnaut, great master of the lore of *love,*
First wrought sestinas to win his lady's *heart,*
Since she was deaf when simpler staves he *sang,*

And for her sake he broke the bonds of *rhyme*,
And in this subtler measure hid his *woe*.

"Harsh be my lines," cried Arnaut, "harsh the *woe*
My lady, that enthorn'd and cruel *rose*,
Inflicts on him that made her live in *rhyme*!"
But through the metre spake the voice of *Love*,
And like a wildwood nightingale he *sang*
Who thought in crabbed lays to ease his *heart*.

It is not told if her untoward *heart*
Was melted by her poet's lyric *woe*,
Or if in vain so amorously he *sang*.
Perchance through cloud of dark conceits he *rose*
To nobler heights of philosophic *love*,
And crowned his later years with sterner *rhyme*.

This thing alone we know: the triple *rhyme*
Of him who bared his vast and passionate *heart*
To all the crossing flames of hate and *love*,
Wears in the midst of all its storm and *woe*—
As some loud morn of March may bear a *rose*—
The impress of a song that Arnaut *sang*.

"Smith of his mother-tongue," the Frenchman *sang*
Of Lancelot and of Galahad, the *rhyme*
That beat so bloodlike at its core of *rose*,
It stirred the sweet Francesca's gentle *heart*
To take that kiss that brought her so much *woe*
And sealed in fire her martyrdom of *love*.

And Dante, full of her immortal *love*,
Stayed his drear song, and softly, fondly *sang*
As though his voice broke with that weight of *woe*;
And to this day we think of Arnaut's *rhyme*
Whenever pity at the labouring *heart*
On fair Francesca's memory drops the *rose*.

Ah, sovereign *Love*, forgive this weaker *rhyme*!
The men of old who *sang* were great at *heart*,
Yet have we too known *woe*, and worn thy *rose*.

—Edmund Gosse

In the following example the closing order is 2 ———— 1, 4 ———— 3, 6 ———— 5. Note the family of end words: *off, on, light, dark, form, remember*.

ON THE WAY HOME FROM NOWHERE, NEW YEAR'S EVE

For papers I think I need, we bump off
the street and stop. I leave the engine on,
mean to make my way to the buzzing light
above the back door, but the door is dark.
Old Main's a hulking, dull, uncertain form,
no windows and no size. Then I remember

one small truth I didn't mean to remember,
that all the lights at ten would be turned off
for somebody's purpose. I enter the hollow form,
try one time to flick the light switch on
and shrug my way into the seamless dark.
What outside seemed scattered, useless light

would be a brilliance here. Reflections. Moonlight.
Sensing my way between the walls I remember
old mythologies of daytime and the dark
spun by gods and monster movies, cast off
with ignorance. My fingers stumble on
another switch. Nothing. I feel my form

falling away into another form.
I hear the hound, look for the quick light
glancing out of his eyes and imagine my own
open, aimless, milky. I remember
what children think of when the lights are off.
Something brushing the hand. To fit the dark

I tell myself I am blind. In such a dark
I could be moving down the spaceless form
of time, a painted tunnel. I twist off
my shoes and walk in deafness. Leap. Grow light
for one slow moment, then loose parts remember
gravity. I twist the sounds back on.

I'm over a million years old and going on
thirteen. I've always been afraid of the dark.
There truly are warlocks, witches, and I remember
banshees, saints and the always shifting form
of Satan himself. I feel a fly light
and crawl across my forehead. I brush it off.

Going on, I grab some papers off
some desk in the dark and turn back toward the light
I barely remember, running, hungry for form.

                                             —Miller Williams

Bruce Taylor's sestina shows the softening of form that we see in
much contemporary patterned poetry, as the line lengths vary in
stress count from three to six, while the pattern of word repetition
through the six sestets is strictly traditional and the end words belong
to the same arena of discourse: *debts, dying, understand, regret, time,
mystery*. Note how the last one can encompass the other five. The closing sequence is 1 ——— 5, 4 ——— 3, 2 ——— 6.

HE LUGS THE GUTS INTO THE OTHER ROOM
Hamlet, Act III, Scene iv

    Time was a son would pay a father's debts,
keep close to ease a father's dying,
have sons himself to teach and understand
how to let go without regret
of everyone we love, one at a time
or all at once, that mystery.

    This is another time, so little mystery
I am a son who hasn't honored my debt
to your sacrifice, all your lost time.
I lived so you could start your dying
and here's the usual regret,
a lack of touch or talk enough to understand.

    Your rage and absences I tried to understand,
your weakness seemed a mystery,
the early marriage and the late regret.

The job you hated but it paid the debts
paid weekly for your daily dying.
You spent yourself in time.

  Early to an empty bed to rise on time
you woke to sunless rooms. I understand
the crush of sequence now, how months go dying
into years, the lack of mystery.
How the future's looming unengendered debts
infect the past with a cancerous regret.

  The past is over. We go beyond regret
to put each other at ease. It's time
to honor you though honor pays no debts
as doesn't praise you wouldn't understand.
Why we did what we did remains a mystery
unsolved by either of our dyings.

  I wasn't there to ease you in your dying.
We die alone and that we all regret,
pass from mystery unto mystery,
our clockwork hearts on borrowed time
live just long enough to understand
to whom we owe and why the heavy debt.

Debts we dread to owe the most, in time
get paid without regret. Sons grow to understand
the living in the dying, the father's mystery.

                                        —Bruce Taylor

    Michael Heffernan's sestina adheres to a five-stress line, unlike the
preceding poem, but the end words belong less clearly to a common
center of concern. Still, there is no sense of disjunction between any
of the words; they work quite comfortably together and are easily (and
progressively) construed as having common cause. The ending sequence is 1 ——— 2, 4 ——— 6, 5 ——— 3.

WORD FROM UNDER

You watch an old dog drowsing in the weather,
a dull dog doing absolutely nothing,

brown rubbish in a leafpile barely breathing
that evidently will incline to lie there
the rest of today and maybe all day tomorrow
letting her life drift emptily down to zero.

This probably chastens the soul, to commune with zero
as an abiding presence in the weather,
neither plus nor minus, and to renounce tomorrow
as a pronounced improvement upon nothing
beyond some blind propensity to lie there
stiffly beneath the air and to keep on breathing

if only because you happen to be breathing,
having acquired such intimacy with zero
and known the solitude of those that lie there
expecting little but the daily weather,
that every effort is a kind of nothing
done for the sake of lasting until tomorrow.

But she is alive today and not tomorrow
and yet displays an aimless way of breathing,
marking her place there like a lump of nothing
precisely in the middle of the round world's zero.
Jaybirds bicker above her, while the weather
bleakly reviles her: "How can you lie there

like any wreckage that would have to lie there
soiling the scenery well beyond tomorrow?
You will grow rotten with redundance." Whether
or not she listens, she persists in breathing
as if, because she has begun with zero
or something like it that is all but nothing,

she has discovered how to live on nothing
and grown good at it so that she can lie there
blank as the genius that invented Zero.
This is the lesson that she leaves: tomorrow
you will attempt to empty your life by breathing
everything out of you into whatever weather

the weather has taken shape as and conceive of nothing.
All you must do is lie there with your mind a zero
and begin the next tomorrow by not breathing.

—Michael Heffernan

DOUBLE BALLADE WITH EIGHT-LINE STANZA. French in origin. A forty-eight-line poem, rhymed like the BALLADE with the final line of each stanza a refrain. Sometimes, but not necessarily, there is an envoy. Lines are syllabic, though in English the measure tends to be iambic, and of any (but equal) length. As with the BALLADE, no rhyme is to be repeated throughout the poem. The rhyme pattern for each stanza is ababbcbC. The envoy, when present, is rhymed bcbC. There is also a *double ballade with a ten-line stanza*, for which the rhyme sequence is ababbccdcD.

William Ernest Henley was particularly fond of the double ballade, varying the form freely to suit his needs.

DOUBLE BALLADE OF LIFE AND FATE

Fools may pine, and sots may swill,
Cynics gibe and prophets rail,
Moralists may scourge and drill,
Preachers prose, and fainthearts quail.
Let them whine, or threat, or wail!
Till the touch of Circumstance
Down to darkness sink the scale,
Fate's a fiddler, Life's a dance.

What if skies be wan and chill?
What if winds be harsh and stale?
Presently the east will thrill,
And the sad and shrunken sail,
Bellying with a kindly gale,
Bear you sunwards, while your chance
Sends you back the hopeful hail!—
"Fate's a fiddler, Life's a dance."

Idle shot or coming bill,
Hapless love or broken bail,

Gulp it (never chew your pill!),
And, if Burgundy should fail,
Try the humbler pot of ale!
Over all is heaven's expanse.
Gold's to find among the shale.
Fate's a fiddler, Life's a dance.

Dull Sir Joskin sleeps his fill,
Good Sir Galahad seeks the Grail,
Proud Sir Pertinax flaunts his frill,
Hard Sir Aeger dints his mail;
And the while by hill and dale
Tristram's braveries gleam and glance,
And his blithe horn tells its tale—
"Fate's a fiddler, Life's a dance."

Araminta's grand and shrill,
Delia's passionate and frail,
Doris drives an earnest quill,
Athanasia takes the veil;
Wiser Phyllis o'er her pail,
At the heart of all romance
Reading, sings to Strephon's flail—
"Fate's a fiddler, Life's a dance."

Every Jack must have his Jill
(Even Johnson had his Thrale!);
Forward, couples—with a will!
This, the world, is not a jail.
Hear the music, sprat and whale!
Hands across, retire, advance!
Though the doomsman's on your trail,
Fate's a fiddler, Life's a dance.

ENVOY

Boys and girls, at slug and snail
And their kindred look askance.
Pay your footing on the nail;
Fate's a fiddler, Life's a dance.

—William Ernest Henley

CHANT ROYAL. French in origin. A sixty-line version of the BAL-
LADE, divided into five stanzas of eleven lines each and a five-line final
stanza, or envoy. Lines are of any (but equal) length and accentual,
though in English they tend to be iambic. The rhyme pattern for the
long stanzas is abcbecddedE. For the envoy the rhyme sequence is
ddedE, as it picks up the last five rhymes of the long stanza. As with
all forms of the BALLADE, no rhyme word is to be repeated throughout
the poem.

BEHOLD THE DEEDS!

(Being the Plaint of Adolphe Culpepper Ferguson, Salesman
of Fancy Notions, held in durance of his Landlady for a failure
to connect on Saturday night)

I would that all men my hard case might know;
    How grievously I suffer for no sin;
I, Adolphe Culpepper Ferguson, for lo!
    I, of my landlady am locked in,
        For being short on this sad Saturday,
        Nor having shekels of silver wherewith to pay;
She has turned and is departed with my key;
Wherefore, not even as other boarders free,
    I sing (as prisoners to their dungeon stones
When for ten days they expiate a spree):
    Behold the deeds that are done of Mrs. Jones!

One night and one day I have wept my woe;
    Nor wot I when the morrow doth begin,
If I shall have to write to Briggs & Co.,
    To pray them to advance the requisite tin
        For ransom of their salesman, that he may
        Go forth as other boarders go alway—
As those I hear now flocking from their tea,
Led by the daughter of my landlady
    Piano-ward. This day, for all my moans,
Dry bread and water have been served me.
    Behold the deeds that are done of Mrs. Jones!

Miss Amabel Jones is musical, and so
    The heart of the young he-boarder doth win,
Playing "The Maiden's Prayer," *adagio*—

That fetcheth him, as fetcheth the banco skin
   The innocent rustic. For my part, I pray:
   That Badarjewska maid may wait for aye
Ere she sits with a lover, as did we
Once sit together, Amabel! Can it be
   That all that arduous wooing not atones
For Saturday shortness of trade dollars three?
   Behold the deeds that are done of Mrs. Jones!

Yea! she forgets the arm was wont to go
   Around her waist. She wears a buckle whose pin
Galleth the crook of the young man's elbów;
   I forget not, for I that youth have been.
     Smith was aforetime the Lothario gay.
     Yet once, I mind me, Smith was forced to stay
Close in his room. Not calm, as I, was he:
But his noise brought no pleasaunce, verily.
   Small ease he gat of playing on the bones,
Or hammering on the stove-pipe, that I see.
   Behold the deeds that are done of Mrs. Jones!

Thou, for whose fear the figurative crow
   I eat, accursed be thou and all thy kin!
Thee will I shew up—yea, up will I shew
   Thy too thick buckwheats, and thy tea too thin.
     Ay! here I dare thee, ready for the fray!
     Thou dost *not* "keep a first-class house," I say!
It does not with the advertisements agree.
Thou lodgest a Briton with a puggaree,
   And thou hast harboured Jacobses and Cohns,
Also a Mulligan. Thus denounce I thee!
   Behold the deeds that are done of Mrs. Jones!

      ENVOY

Boarders; the worst I have not told to ye:
She hath stolen my trousers, that I may not flee
   Privily by the window. Hence these groans,
There is no fleeing in a robe de nuit.
   Behold the deeds that are done of Mrs. Jones!
              —Henry Cuyler Bunner

The sense of closure in the following chant royal is strengthened by terminal alteration of the refrain.

REQUIEM FOR THE OLD PROFESSOR

> The day dawned when his scholar's armament
>   Grew thin as rust. A crust of lacy mold
> Lay thick upon his lectures in the tent,
>   Weathered by lost crusades, that let the cold
> Sigh in through rents and fissures. Now the mailed
> Fist loosened, lost its grip. His standard swaled
>   And fell in tatters to lie upon the green,
>   Abandoned sward that had been his demesne—
>   The Groves of Academe. He would avoid
> This final joust if some way might be seen;
>   Alas! the old professor is destroyed.
>
> He saw the horseman pale upon a bent
>   And bony courser—as had been foretold
> In many an ancient tome and document—
>   Hover into view: Death held a rolled
> Parchment summons. As he rode he flailed
> The air with a crescent edge—the blade was tailed
>   With a long, thin handle carved and serpentine.
>   The wind began to rise, to sough and keen;
>   Steel must meet steel in combat unalloyed
> By mettle that is base or in-between—
>   Alas! the old professor is destroyed.
>
> The spectres of the hosts that he had sent
>   Into the world, girded with lore and bold
> With youth, began to gather, each intent
>   Upon this field of combat, for he had doled
> His learning out among them but had regaled
> None with tales of wisdom. Nor had he railed
>   In passion at their phlegm, their lack of spleen,
>   For he had aimed his point against their mean.
>   His tun of ordinary mead had cloyed
> With age, become the Ambrosia-That-Might-Have-Been.
>   Alas! the old professor is destroyed.

Now his lance is lowered; his sands are spent,
   Gone siling down the glass. His quivering hold
Upon the haft is weak. His lungs give vent
   To one last battlecry. He has cajoled
This steed of hours into a trot, assailed
The Knight of Darkness—at least he has not quailed
   Before his sure defeat: it is a clean
   Break with the flesh, this ultimate careen
     Against the foe that he could not avoid.
   He lifts his buckler and begins to lean—
     Alas! the old professor is destroyed.

Let us abandon tropes, say what is meant
   In clear, spare language so that we may hold
The old professor to the light. He went
   The way that all flesh goes; first, he told
Himself that he would seek the Grail. He failed.
He found preferments, tenure, and he nailed
   His sheepskin to the wall, then mailed a lean
   Listing of his honors to the dean
     Who filed it in a folder labeled *Void*.
That's all there was. He faded from the scene.
     At last the old professor is destroyed.

Here lies a man benighted. What may we glean
From his demise and tale? Alack! I ween
   There is but little here to be enjoyed—
We join the host of phantoms who convene
     To see the old professor is destroyed.

                      —Wesli Court

SONNET REDOUBLÉ. French in origin. Fifteen SONNETS of any type tied together by the fact that each line of the first sonnet becomes, in its turn, the last line of one of the following fourteen.

REFLECTIONS IN AN ATTIC ROOM:
A SONNET REDOUBLÉ

As if one needed to begin to write;
As though one had to have a pen at hand,

Paper smoothening to the touch of night,
Light sifting across the page like wind and sand.

This is the scrivener's fallacy, the hour
Abraded by sand and wind, by wilful words:
They scrape at vision, they scarify and scour—
The urn becomes a scuttering of shards;

The wind, a voice freed of its hollow shell
Noting nothings echoing in the bone
Bleaching among the dunes of time that swell:
They shift, remembering they once were stone.

Sit stony-eyed; watch the words curl and come
Stillborn to light between the joint and thumb.

Dear father:
          You are dead. What's there to say?
Yet I'll go on to say it, as you know,
Or may not, as the case may be. Just so,
Our monologues continue on their way.
Two streams of silence rising out of clay,
Passing each other in the essential flow
Of stars and atoms. Watch them rise and go,
Falling in vortices of night and day:

The grass grows green, the suns and planets turn
Upon a field of darkness. Brine turns to blood,
I turn to you as day turns into night,
As flesh turns in to earth. I cannot spurn
The flame you gave to me upon the flood
As if one needed to begin.
                              To write

Is useless. "Poetry makes nothing happen,"
As Auden said. It happens anyhow,
Rising upon the eternal tide of now,
Engulfing everything—the field, the aspen,
Herb, rock, and furrow. So we sigh, grasp pen,
Ink and paper, then we sit down to plow

Another row of letters. We endow
The meadow with another seed to open.

And when it does, what will the blossom be?
Another flower in a sea of flowers?
A blooming and a withering of the land
That once was ocean, that once more shall be sea
Rising to blood again to invest these hours
As though one had to have a pen at hand?

Here in an attic study rising to
A peak in the winter dark, one thinks at times
Of love; one thinks of synonyms and rhymes
That come as close as words are wont to do
To what it once was like when the flesh was new
And closed with flesh in torrid zones and climes.
What was it like? Whose were those pantomimes,
Between the sheets, that got the rave reviews?

Those sheets—those wrinkled sheets: they press in close
Upon recall. The books that line these shelves
Are filled with love yellowing and trite:
Verbena pressed between the leaves verbose.
Our sheets untwine, leaving to our selves
Paper smoothening to the touch of night.

The attic listens to the scratching pen.
Outdoors, the wind has sunk. The snow is deep,
The neighbors in their steads are fast asleep,
Dreaming of when they will awake again.
Nothing is happening, nor will it when
They lift their lids to look into the deep
Trance of wakening. The ink will keep
The stillness that inhabits books and men,

Will keep it and disgorge it as the leaf
Turns, veined and sere, and then begins to brown
Under the rooftree, beneath the moving hand.
The words accumulate, become a sheaf

Of seasons as the silence filters down,
Light sifting across the page like wind and sand.

Imagine this: a battering at the door;
The voice of anguish pleading, "Give us curds,
Crusts, crumbs of meaning—pray you, give us words!
We need the Secret Name, and so much more—
A sense of purpose from your ample store
Of synonyms and antonyms! Rewards
Undreamt await if you extend towards
Your fellow man a portion of your lore!"

But the knocker lies against the stolid wood;
The panel does not echo. The empty hall
Contains but peeling paper and a sour
Smell of waiting. It must be understood
There is no understanding, only gall:
This is the scrivener's fallacy.
                                        The hour

Is late. The atmosphere is thick. The earth
Is running down. The fishes in the sea
Are drowned in silt. Each blade of grass, each tree
Is blighted. There has been a monstrous birth,
And plenitude has been transformed to dearth—
The Magi slouch away from Galilee.
"The pen is mightier than the sword," but see
It beaten into shares of slender worth:

It settles in its rut and plows its row.
The poisonous sun and parching raindrops slough
From brow and temple. Emaciated birds,
Before the wrinkled seed can sprout and grow,
Seize it for ivied towers wearing down,
Abraded by sand and wind, by wilful words.

Go, little book, and bear thy wordy freight
Away from me as fast as e'er thou may—
I'm sick to death of everything you say.

I wrote you out in sundry hours late
When I long since ought to have hit the hay—
But did I seek sweet dreaming? Did I sate
The wingéd Pegasus at an early date,
In a timely moment? Nay, I say you, neigh!

I entertained the nightmare in my room.
I watched that grim old nag bend to devour
The grain of bitterness, the oats of doom,
The silage of depression. Little, sour
Book, I loathe thy messages of gloom—
They scrape at vision, they scarify and scour.

Build me more stately vessels, O my soul!
I have a pot to piss in, sure enough,
But I've a fancy for more fancy stuff:
Amphorae full of oils, a wassail bowl,
Kraters of flowers. Ceramics is my goal:
A funerary urn, built good and tough,
Of alabaster so that, when I slough
This clay, my ash won't end up in a hole.

But what is this? I look into my heart
And find a crock chock-full of feeble words;
A thunder-jug beladen with a fart;
Stained paper, and a nest of nestling turds—
And as I watch, the paper falls apart;
The urn becomes a scuttering of shards.

I wrote a book called *Curses and Laments*.
There was, it seems, a modicum of scents
In such an exercise, but only that:
A modicum, for it relieves frustration,
But changes nothing else in God's creation.
You pucker up and whistle in your hat;
You break a little wind when you're intense—
I wrote a book called *Curses and Laments*.

You take a certain pleasure in the smell
Of fire and brimstone. They can go to Hell,

Those bastards that have muscled you around.
Leave them a curse and then go underground
To breathe the air where you have loosed to swell
The wind a voice freed of its hollow shell.

What do we talk about beneath the stone?
"I have a little dust stuck in my eye.
Today the worms are restless. I can feel
Them turning. Pardon me, I have a cold—
I cannot stop my coughing. Thought I'd die
Of laughter when my nasty neighbor went
Out in the rain and caught her death. I saw
Pale Ryder the other day—he's looking old
And out of sorts. I wait for the telephone
To ring, but my children never seem to call.
Perhaps it's out of order—the reaper man
Doesn't service the equipment he has sold."

Perhaps it's much like life—we merely lie
Noting nothings echoing.
                              In bone-

Yards poets slowly accumulate.
I sometimes wonder if, on Judgement Day,
We'll all rise up in glory to afflate,
Converse, and each recite his latest lai.
Can rime be so perverse? In Plato's State
We'd all be banished—even the great Good Gray
Poet. But where in God's name could we go—
To that grand Writers' Conference Below?

But even there we would, it seems to me,
Be welcomed none too warmly to pause or dwell.
There'd be the Devil to pay, inevitably,
For there are limits to tolerance in Hell.
If we are left alone with our poetry
Bleaching among the dunes of time, that's well.

So Limbo's won and Paradise is lost.
My attic room is filling up with smoke:
I sit and talk with Geoffrey, Will—a host

Of my confreres. We pass the time with joke
And bawdry. There is little else to do—
The centuries lie heavy as a yoke

Upon the roof; the cracking of the glue
In all our bindings shatters this still air.
Our words and verse go whistling up the flue.

We pilgrims to perdition sit and stare
Into the silence of sere marrow-bone.
I proffer the hemlock cup—they do not dare

Accept, for if they drank I'd be alone.
They shift, remembering they once were stone.

And in my pipesmoke I can just discern
The outlines of a sonnet redoublé,
A skeleton of what is my concern:
The meaning of it all. My smoke is grey.

I ponder carefully these artful rounds
And think about the things I have to say—
I try some lines aloud. The noise resounds
To my House of Fame, and meters ricochet

From the sloping walls to die upon my ears.
Where are the hare of soul, the baying hounds
Of the Apocalypse? Where are the tears
Condensed from feelings language seldom sounds?

My room is silent; my pen is chill and dumb.
Sit stony-eyed with words that curl and come.

Now it is almost done, this foolish thing
That I have penned. The lines have nearly jelled,
And I must ask if I have felt compelled
To write, or merely willed myself to sing

This song that few will ever care to read.
And was I born, or was I merely made,
Concocted of myself—the man of trade,
Not the Bard God conjured out of need

To cure the universe? I do not care.
To be a poet of whatever sort
Will help to pass this journey to the Court
Of Ultimate Decisions. This is fare

I pay and eat—these lines that fall and come
Stillborn to light between the joint and thumb.

—Wesli Court

4 Traditional Poems of Indefinite Length

CYWYDD DEUAIR HYRION (cuh'-with day'-air her'-yon). Welsh in origin. Popularized by the poet Dafydd ap Gwylym in the fourteenth century. It endures as a popular form among contemporary Welsh poets. The cywydd is comprised of any number of rhyming couplets of seven syllables each with the accentuation differing on the rhyming words. This is best seen in the following example.

LAMENT FOR OWAIN AB URIEN

Owain ab Urien's soul
May the Lord keep immortal.
Lordly to praise Rheged's lord,
Greatly burdened by greensward,
Laid low, this far-bruited king,
His lances wings of dawning.
To none other was he thrall,
No other was his equal,
Reaper of foes, ravener,
Son, father, and grandfather.
When Owain scythed down Fflamddwynn
It was no more than nodding.
Sleeping are the Anglemen,
Light in their sockets open,
And those who but shortly fled
Were bolder than they needed—
Owain put them to the sack:
Sheep before the wolf-pack.
Grand in colored armament,
Well he horsed the suppliant:
For his soul's sake Owain shared
The treasure that he hoarded.

Owain ab Urien's soul
May the Lord keep immortal.

—Taliesin (Seventh century)

Translated by Wesli Court

CYWYDD DEUAIR FYRION (cuh'-with day'-air fruh'-yon). Welsh in origin. Any number of couplets with four-syllable lines in true or off rhyme.

MY CHOICE

I choose a fair
Maid so slender,
Tall and silver,
Her gown of heather
Hue—I choose her,
Nature's daughter,
For the kind word
Dropped, scarcely heard,
And for my part
Take her to heart
For gift, for grace,
For her embrace.

I choose the wave,
The water's shade;
Witch of the shire,
Your Welsh tongue pure,
My choice you are,
And am I yours?
Why be silent
(Sweet your silence)?
I choose my course
Without remorse,
With a clear voice—
So clear a choice.

—Hywel ab Owain Gwynedd

(Twelfth century)

Translated by Wesli Court

TERZA RIMA. Italian in origin. A poem of any number of three-line stanzas and a terminal couplet or triplet, usually in iambic pentameter, though the lines can be of any (equal) length and in any meter. The full stanzas are interlocked so that the final sound of line 2 of each stanza rhymes with the first and third lines of the following stanza. The resolving couplet or triplet will usually rhyme with the middle rhymed sound of the preceding tercet. Thus, in a five-stanza terza rima the rhyme pattern would be aba, bcb, cdc, ded, ee; or, if the final stanza is a triplet, as in the following example, the pattern would end eee.

> Men marry what they need. I marry you,
> morning by morning, day by day, night by night,
> and every marriage makes this marriage new.
>
> In the broken name of heaven, in the light
> that shatters granite, by the spitting shore,
> in air that leaps and wobbles like a kite,
>
> I marry you from time and a great door
> is shut and stays shut against wind, sea, stone,
> sunburst, and heavenfall. And home once more
>
> inside our walls of skin and struts of bone,
> man-woman, woman-man, and each the other,
> I marry you by all dark and all dawn
>
> and have my laugh at death. Why should I bother
> the flies about me? Let them buzz and do.
> Men marry their queen, their daughter, or their mother
>
> by hidden names, but that thin buzz whines through:
> where reasons are no reason, cause is true.
> Men marry what they need. I marry you.
>
>   —John Ciardi

KYRIELLE. French in origin. Any number of quatrains with lines of eight syllables (though in English the measure tends to become iambic) and any rhyme scheme or none, as the poet chooses. The last line of each stanza is a refrain. The following poem's rhyme pattern thus fits the definition.

KYRIELLE

A little pain, a little pleasure,	a
A little heaping up of treasure,	a
Then no more gazing upon the sun.	b
All things must end that have begun.	B
Where is the time for hope or doubt?	c
A puff of the wind, and life is out;	c
A turn of the wheel, and the rest is won.	b
All things must end that have begun.	B
Golden morning and purple night,	d
Life that fails with the failing light;	d
Death is the only deathless one.	b
All things must end that have begun.	B

—John Payne

PANTOUM. Adopted into French from Malaysian poetry, by Ernest Fouinet. Victor Hugo used it briefly, but few have worked with it since. Any number of quatrains with lines of any (but equal) length and in any meter. Stanzas interlock as lines 2 and 4 of each stanza become lines 1 and 3 of the next. The lines that move as a pair (*i.e.*, the alternate lines, 1 and 3, 2 and 4) are rhymed.

Any interlocking of stanzas presents a problem at the point of resolution, at which there is no following stanza to pick up the linking lines. (See also SESTINA and VILLANELLE, and Frost's poem "Stopping by Woods on a Snowy Evening.") The pantoum is resolved in one of two ways. The final quatrain may reach back and pick up lines 1 and 3 of stanza 1, using them as lines 4 and 2, respectively. Or the last stanza may be a couplet comprised of these two lines, also in reverse order, from the first stanza.

For a four-stanza poem, the pattern is $A_1B_1A_2B_2$, $B_1C_1B_2C_2$, $C_1D_1C_2D_2$, $D_1A_2D_2A_1$. Or if the second option is chosen for the resolution, the final stanza would be A_2A_1.

ALWAYS THE ONE WHO LOVES HIS FATHER MOST

Always the one who loves his father most,
the one the father loves the most in turn,

will fight against his father as he must.
Neither knows what he will come to learn.

The one the father loves the most in turn
tells the father no and no and no,
but neither knows what he will come to learn
nor cares a lot what that could be, and so

tells his father no and no and no,
is ignorant of what the years will teach
nor cares a lot what that could be, and so
unties the knot that matters most, while each

is ignorant of what the years will teach,
they'll learn how pride—if each lives out his years—
unties the knot that matters most, while each
will feel a sadness, feel the midnight fears.

They'll learn how pride—if each lives out his years—
will lose the aging other as a friend,
will feel a sadness, feel the midnight fears.
The child and then the father, world without end,

will lose the aging other as a friend.
And then the child of that one, too, will grow—
the child and then the father, world without end—
in turn to fight his father, *comme il faut,*

will fight against his father, as he must,
always, the one who loves his father most.

—Clement Long

CYHYDEDD NAW BAN (cuh-huh'-death now bawn). Welsh in origin. A poem made up of nine-syllable lines. The rhyme pattern is such
that the poem can be divided into groups of consecutive lines that
rhyme. Each line must be part of such a group, and each group must
consist of at least two lines, though it may consist of many more. For
instance, the rhyme pattern of the first stanza of the following example is aaaabbccdd.

IN PRAISE OF OWAIN GWYNEDD

I hail a boonsman hearty in war,
Battlewolf, boastful, first to the fore—
I sing of serving him with fervor,
Sing his mead-fed and worthy power,
Sing his ardor, this wind-winged falcon,
Sing his thoughts, lofty as the welkin,
Sing his dauntless deeds, lord of frayhounds,
Sing his praises—they may know no bounds,
Sing odes for my magnanimous thane;
I sing paeans of praise for Owain.

Armed for Angles in Tegeingl's realms,
Blood's spouting streams, our blades' spating storms,
We met dragons, the warriors of Rome,
A prince's son—costly their winestream.
Striving with the Dragon of the East
The western Dragon showed which was best.
Lusty our lord, his bright blade unsheathed—
The sword poured forth, the spear was strife-bathed,
Blade in hand and all hands hewing heads,
Hand on hilt and edge on Norman hordes—

At the sight of death, constant wailing
And swashbuckling and loud revelling,
Blood flowing from brave men's riven skulls—
I heard flesh pledged to the birds' bowels
In the fierce thrust of the sharp ash-haft,
In the raven-beckoning blood-path.
On corpses to feed a thousand shrikes
Brynnich's riders rode, Owain's war kites.
Carcasses, carrion by the bushels,
The taste of battle, killed men's entrails!

For his prize we fought, and for his praise,
Hosts and bards, for Owain's bounteous ways,
To Cadell Hiriell Hiriein's scion
For reward, guardian of Coel's line,
Battlefield's lance-thrust, praise-lavishing,
Shield-carrying, eagle onrushing

Court's stalwart, vigilant defender—
Beware his thrusting, three-colored spear!

They harvested Aberteifi's spears
With battlecries, as at Badon Fawr.
I saw war-stags, corpses stiff and red—
We let the fierce wolf put them to bed;
They ran without arms—some without hands,
Mighty warriors under talons;
I saw their rout—three hundred were slain;
I saw bowels on thorns, the war won.
I saw the strife, heard the battleshout,
Saw knights belaboring troops in flight.

I saw men falling from the chalk heights,
The foe slaughtered among their redoubts;
I saw pikes blooming about a wall
And lances rushing at Owain's call—
I saw the charge make Saxon carnage
And princes reaping the day's courage.
Prince of princes! His battle is won,
Bought dearly—he is pursued by none.
I saw at Rhuddlan a ruddy tide,
A hero's host heroic in pride—

I saw in Penfro a prince peerless;
I saw in Penardd a lord fearless;
I saw their slaughter of the doughty
Borne by a brave land, the fern's bounty.
I saw men thronging and scurrying,
Heard alarums, saw troops hurrying,
Saw them taken, saw comrades in pain,
Saw strife near Caer and Coen Llywfain.
Gwynedd's valor was proven again—
You were dauntless, shepherd of Britain!

> —Cynddelw Brydydd Mawr (Twelfth century)
>
> Translated by Wesli Court

CYHYDEDD HIR (cuh-huh'-death here). Welsh in origin. A poem of interrhyming eight-line stanzas composed of two quatrains each. The

lines of the quatrains contain five, five, five, and four syllables respectively; the five-syllable lines rhyme, and the fourth line rhymes with
the fourth line in the next quatrain.

sssss	a
sssss	a
sssss	a
ssss	b
sssss	c
sssss	c
sssss	c
ssss	b
sssss	d
sssss	d
sssss	d
ssss	e
sssss	f
sssss	f
sssss	f
ssss	e

TO A GIRL

I saw on the face
Of a haughty lass
A look with no trace
    Of love—cold, still:
The cresting spume-glow
Upon the billow
Of the sea's face, flow
    And ebb of chill.

She sends her respects
To me, harshly, vexed—
The candle rejects,
    Cuts shadow dead,
And now I must hoard
Disgrace's great hurt—

She's trod on my heart,
 Sought Greeneye's bed!
  —Cynddelw Brydydd Mawr
    (Twelfth century)
     Translated by Wesli Court

RHUPUNT. Welsh in origin. A poem of interrhyming stanzas of three, four, or five lines with each line containing four syllables. All but the last line rhyme, which last line rhymes with the last line in the following stanza in pairs.

A rhupunt can also be a single line of three, four, or five sections with each section having four syllables. All but the last section rhyme, which last section rhymes with the last section in the following line in pairs.

The formula given below is for the first definition, using four-line stanzas.

s s s s	a
s s s s	a
s s s s	a
s s s s	b
s s s s	c
s s s s	c
s s s s	c
s s s s	b
s s s s	d
s s s s	d
s s s s	d
s s s s	e
s s s s	f
s s s s	f
s s s s	f
s s s s	e

A RIDDLE

Riddle me this—
Knew the Flood's kiss,

Has a snake's hiss,
This great creature,

Fleshless, boneless,
Senseless, bloodless,
Headless, footless,
Older nor younger

Then he started,
Never daunted,
Not live nor dead,
Ever useful—

God in Heaven,
What origin?
Great wonders Thine
Who made this bull.

In woods, in leas,
Ageless, griefless,
Ever hurtless,
Of equal age

With the Eras,
Older than hours
From Time's ewers;
Broad as the gauge

Of all the earth.
He had no birth,
Nor has he girth
On land or sea.

Trust him to hum—
He will lie dumb
And will not come
If it need be.

Bull of the air
Beyond compare,
None may ensnare
Him in his den

On the sea-cliff.
He'll roar, he'll cough,
Mannerless oaf—
Savage again

Crossing the land
Roaring and grand,
Then hushed and bland,
Fey as a boy,

Then with a shout
Lashing about
Earth is a rout.
Wickedness, joy,

Hidden yet seen
In his careen,
Heard in his whine
First here, then there,

Hurling, twirling,
Ever breaking,
Never paying
Bull of the air.

Blameless as sky,
He is wet, dry,
Often comes by.
Old Man-fashioned,

Like everything
From beginning
Unto ending—
He is the wind.

—Anonymous

(*ca.* Tenth century)

Translated by Wesli Court

ENGLISH ODE. Obviously English in origin, but simply a combination of the SICILIAN QUATRAIN and an Italian sestet. A poem comprised of any number of ten-line stanzas, rhymed (with different rhymes for each stanza) as follows. Traditionally iambic. Five-stress lines. Lewis Turco sees the form as a wedding of the English and Italian SONNETS.

⌣ /	⌣ /	⌣ /	⌣ /	⌣ /	a
⌣ /	⌣ /	⌣ /	⌣ /	⌣ /	b
⌣ /	⌣ /	⌣ /	⌣ /	⌣ /	a
⌣ /	⌣ /	⌣ /	⌣ /	⌣ /	b
⌣ /	⌣ /	⌣ /	⌣ /	⌣ /	c
⌣ /	⌣ /	⌣ /	⌣ /	⌣ /	d
⌣ /	⌣ /	⌣ /	⌣ /	⌣ /	e
⌣ /	⌣ /	⌣ /	⌣ /	⌣ /	c
⌣ /	⌣ /	⌣ /	⌣ /	⌣ /	d
⌣ /	⌣ /	⌣ /	⌣ /	⌣ /	e

ODE TO A NIGHTINGALE

I

My heart aches, and a drowsy numbness pains
　My sense, as though of hemlock I had drunk,
Or emptied some dull opiate to the drains
　One minute past, and Lethe-wards had sunk:
'Tis not through envy of thy happy lot,
　But being too happy in thine happiness,—
　　That thou, light-winged Dryad of the trees,
　　　In some melodious plot
　Of beechen green, and shadows numberless,
　　Singest of summer in full-throated ease.

II

O, for a draught of vintage! that hath been
　Cool'd a long age in the deep-delved earth,
Tasting of Flora and the country green,
　Dance, and Provençal song, and sunburnt mirth!
O for a beaker full of the warm South,
　Full of the true, the blushful Hippocrene,
　　With beaded bubbles winking at the brim,
　　　And purple-stained mouth;
　That I might drink, and leave the world unseen,
　　And with thee fade away into the forest dim:

III

Fade far away, dissolve, and quite forget
  What thou among the leaves hast never known,
The weariness, the fever, and the fret
  Here, where men sit and hear each other groan;
Where palsy shakes a few, sad, last gray hairs,
    Where youth grows pale, and spectre-thin, and dies;
      Where but to think is to be full of sorrow
        And leaden-eyed despairs,
    Where Beauty cannot keep her lustrous eyes,
      Or new Love pine at them beyond to-morrow.

IV

Away! away! for I will fly to thee,
  Not charioted by Bacchus and his pards,
But on the viewless wings of Poesy,
  Though the dull brain perplexes and retards:
Already with thee! tender is the night
  And haply the Queen-Moon is on her throne,
    Cluster'd around by all her starry Fays;
      But here there is no light,
  Save what from heaven is with the breezes blown
    Through verdurous glooms and winding mossy ways.

V

I cannot see what flowers are at my feet,
  Nor what soft incense hangs upon the boughs,
But, in embalmed darkness, guess each sweet
  Wherewith the seasonable month endows
The grass, the thicket, and the fruit-tree wild;
    White hawthorn, and the pastoral eglantine;
      Fast fading violets cover'd up in leaves;
        And mid-May's eldest child,
  The coming musk-rose, full of dewy wine,
    The murmurous haunt of flies on summer eves.

VI

Darkling I listen; and, for many a time
  I have been half in love with easeful Death,
Call'd him soft names in many a mused rhyme,

To take into the air my quiet breath;
Now more than ever seems it rich to die,
   To cease upon the midnight with no pain,
     While thou art pouring forth thy soul abroad
       In such an ectasy!
   Still wouldst thou sing, and I have ears in vain—
    To thy high requiem become a sod.

VII

Thou wast not born for death, immortal Bird!
   No hungry generations tread thee down;
The voice I hear this passing night was heard
   In ancient days by emperor and clown:
Perhaps the self-same song that found a path
    Through the sad heart of Ruth, when, sick for home,
     She stood in tears amid the alien corn;
      The same that oft-times hath
   Charm'd magic casements, opening on the foam
    Of perilous seas, in faery lands forlorn.

VIII

Forlorn! the very word is like a bell
   To toll me back from thee to my sole self!
Adieu! the fancy cannot cheat so well
   As she is fam'd to do, deceiving elf.
Adieu! adieu! thy plaintive anthem fades
    Past the near meadows, over the still stream,
     Up the hill-side; and now 'tis buried deep
      In the next valley-glades:
   Was it a vision, or a waking dream?
    Fled is that music:—Do I wake or sleep?

                    —John Keats

PINDARIC ODE. Derived from the Greek. A poem in three parts: the *turn*, or *strophe*; the *counterturn*, or *antistrophe*; and the *stand*, or *epode*. The meter, line length, and stanza length are determined by the poet.

The patterns of the first two sections are identical and different from that of the third. It is impossible to extrapolate a general formula for the Pindaric ode; an example will serve.

PINDARIC ODE

To the Immortal Memory and
Friendship of That Noble
Pair, Sir Lucius Cary and
Sir H. Morrison

1. THE TURN

It is not growing like a tree
In bulk, doth make men better be;
Or standing long an oak, three hundred year,
To fall a log at last, dry, bald, and sear:
A lily of a day
Is fairer far, in May,
Although it fall and die that night;
It was the plant and flower of light.
In small proportions we just beauties see;
And in short measures life may perfect be.

2. THE COUNTER-TURN

Call, noble Lucius, then for wine,
And let thy looks with gladness shine;
Accept this garland, plant it on thy head,
And think, nay know, thy Morrison's not dead.
He leap'd the present age,
Possess'd with holy rage,
To see that bright eternal day
Of which we priests and poets say
Such truths as we expect for happy men:
And there he lives with memory, and Ben.

3. THE STAND

Jonson, who sung this of him, ere he went,
Himself, to rest,
Or taste a part of that full joy he meant
To have express'd,
In this bright asterism!—
Where it were friendship's schism,
Were not his Lucius long with us to tarry,
To separate these twi-
Lights, the Dioscuri;
And keep the one half from his Harry.

But fate doth so alternate the design,
Whilst that in heav'n, this light on earth must shine.

—Ben Jonson

BLANK VERSE. Classical in origin. It was introduced into English by William Surrey and soon became the major form in the language. It consists of any number of lines of unrhymed iambic pentameter. The unrhymed looser five-stress line of some contemporary poets is now often referred to as blank verse. In iambics, the lines are shown as follows.

∪ /   ∪ /   ∪ /   ∪ /   ∪ /   x
∪ /   ∪ /   ∪ /   ∪ /   ∪ /   x

From 1 HENRY IV: *Act III, Scene ii*

PRINCE: So please your majesty, I would I could
Quit all offenses with as clear excuse
As well as I am doubtless I can purge
Myself of many I am charged withal;
Yet such extenuation let me beg,
As, in reproof of many tales devised
(Which oft the ear of greatness needs must hear)
By smiling pickthanks and base newsmongers,
I may, for some things true, wherein my youth
Hath faulty wandered and irregular,
Find pardon on my true submission.

KING: God pardon thee; yet let me wonder, Harry,
At thy affections, which do hold a wing
Quite from the flight of all thy ancestors.
Thy place in council thou hast rudely lost,
Which by thy younger brother is supplied,
And art almost an alien to the hearts
Of all the court and princes of my blood.
The hope and expectation of thy time
Is ruined, and the soul of every man
Prophetically do forethink thy fall.
Had I so lavish of my presence been,

So common-hackneyed in the eyes of men,
So stale and cheap to vulgar company,
Opinion, that did help me to the crown,
Had still kept loyal to possessión
And left me in reputeless banishment,
A fellow of no mark nor likelihood.

—William Shakespeare

From PARADISE LOST

Of man's first disobedience, and the fruit
Of that forbidden tree whose mortal taste
Brought death into the world, and all our woe,
With loss of Eden, till one greater Man
Restore us, and regain the blissful seat,
Sing, Heavenly Muse, that, on the secret top
Of Oreb, or of Sinai, didst inspire
That shepherd who first taught the chosen seed
In the beginning how the Heavens and Earth
Rose out of Chaos: or, if Sion hill
Delight thee more, and Siloa's brook that flowed
Fast by the oracle of God, I thence
Invoke thy aid to my adventurous song,
That with no middle flight intends to soar
Above th' Aonian mount, while it pursues
Things unattempted yet in prose or rhyme.

—John Milton

STORM WINDOWS

People are putting up storm windows now,
Or were, this morning, until the heavy rain
Drove them indoors. So, coming home at noon,
I saw storm windows lying on the ground,
Frame-full of rain; through the water and glass
I saw the crushed grass, how it seemed to stream
Away in lines like seaweed on the tide
Or blades of wheat leaning under the wind.
The ripple and splash of rain on the blurred glass

Seemed that it briefly said, as I walked by,
Something I should have liked to say to you,
Something . . . the dry grass bent under the pane
Brimful of bouncing water . . . something of
A swaying clarity which blindly echoes
This lonely afternoon of memories
And missed desires, while the wintry rain
(Unspeakable, the distance in the mind!)
Runs on the standing windows and away.

—Howard Nemerov

ANGLO-SAXON VERSE. Any number of four-stress lines with me-
dial caesuras, with a syllable in the first half of the line being allit-
erative with one in the second half. The form in which the great
Anglo-Saxon poems were written. *Judith*, one of the extant poems dating from Anglo-Saxon times, has been rendered into English by Ann
Babb with remarkable fidelity to the shape and sound of the original.
These are the closing lines.

Those who had been
Most hateful in life   of living peoples
Lay dead on the field.   The victory-folk
Came back to Bethulia   their bright city
Within the month.   Those illustrious men
Carried to Judith,   courageous lady,
Helmets and hip-swords,   the armor of heroes
Adorned with gold,   grey corselets,
Most precious gems   than any man
Can ever reckon.   Heroic warriors,
Brave under banners,   had won this booty
By courage in battle,   on account of Judith,
Stout-hearted woman,   wise of counsel.
They offered her Holofernus'
Bloody corselet;   his helmet and broadsword
With red gold tracings;   and all his treasure,
The gold and jewels   gathered up
By that haughty prince   in his pride and insolence.
This wealth was given   to Judith the wise,

To Judith the famed.   She called that fortune
Glory to God,   Who gave her honor
Both here on earth   and in Heaven.
He rewarded her feat,   for she had faith
In the Lord of Hosts   and truly believed
That she would rise   to the realm of Heaven.
Praise His Name   forevermore,
The Lord God,   Who in His grace
Made wind and air,   and stormy waters
And land and sky,   and Heaven's joys.

   Fred Chappell has turned his hand to the form for one of his own
poems.

MY GRANDFATHER'S CHURCH GOES UP
                    (Acts 2: 1–47)

God is a fire in the head.
            —Nijinsky

Holocaust, pentecost: what heaped heartbreak:

The tendrils of fire   forthrightly tasting
foundation to rooftree   flesh of that edifice . . .
Why was sear sent   to sunder those jointures,
the wheat-hued wood   wasted to heaven?
Both altar and apse   the air ascended
in sullen smoke.
                    (It was surely no sign
of God's salt grievance   but grizzled Weird grimly
and widely wandering.)
                    The dutiful worshipers
stood afar ghast-struck   as the green cedar shingles
burst outward like birds   disturbed in their birling.
Choir stall crushed inward   flayed planking in curlicues
back on it bending,   broad beams of chestnut
oak poplar and pine   gasht open paint-pockets.
And the organ uttered   an unholy Omega
as gilt pipes and pedals   pulsed into rubble.

How it all took tongue!   A total hosannah
this building burgeoned,   the black hymnals whispering
leaves lisping in agony   leaping alight,
sopranos' white scapulars   each singly singeing
robes of the baritones   roaring like rivers
the balcony bellowing   and buckling. In the basement
where the M.Y.F.   had mumbled for mercies
the cane-bottomed chairs   chirruped Chinese.
What a glare   of garish glottals
rose from the nave   what knar-mouth natter!
And the transept tottered   intoning like tympani
as the harsh heat   held hold there.
The whole church resounded   reared its rare anthem
crying out Christ-mercy   to the cloud-cloven sky.

Those portents Saint Paul   foretold to us peoples
fresh now appeared: bifurcate fire-tongues,
and as of wild winds   a swart mighty wrestling,
blood fire and vapor   of smoke vastly vaulting,
the sun into darkness   deadened and dimmed,
wonders in heaven   signs wrought in the world:
the Spirit poured out   on souls of us sinners.
In this din as of drunkenness   the old men dreamed dreams,
the daughters and sons   supernal sights saw.
God's gaudy grace   grasped them up groaning.
Doubt parched within them   pure power overtaking
their senses. Sobbing   like sweethearts bereft
the brothers and sisters   burst into singing.
Truly the Holy   Ghost here now halted,
held sway in their hearts   healed there the hurt.

Now over the narthex   the neat little steeple
force of the fire   felt furiously.
Bruit of black smoke   borne skyward
shadowed its shutters   swam forth in swelter.
It stood as stone   for onstreaming moments
then carefully crumpled   closed inward in char.
The brass bell within it   broke loose, bountifully

pealing, plunged   plangent to the pavement
and a glamour of clangor   gored cloudward gaily.

That was the ringing that wrung   remorse out of us clean,
the elemental echo   the elect would hear always;
in peace or in peril   that peal would pull them.

Seventeen seasons   have since parted
the killing by fire   of my grandfather's kirk.
Moving of our Maker   on this middle earth
is not to be mind-gripped   by any men.

Here Susan and I   saw it, come
to this wood, wicker   basket and wool blanket
swung between us,   in sweet June
on picnic. Prattling   like parakeets
we smoothed out for our meal-place   the mild meadow grasses
and spread our sandwiches   in the sunlit greensward.
Then amorously ate.   And afterward
lay languorous and   looking lazily.
Green grass and pokeweed   gooseberry bushes
pink rambling rose   and raspberry vine
sassafras and thistle   and serrate sawbriar
clover and columbine   clung to the remnants,
grew in that ground   once granted to God.
Blackbirds and thrushes   built blithely there
the ferret and kingsnake   fed in the footing.
The wilderness rawly   had walked over those walls
and the deep-drinking forest   driven them down.

Now silence sang: swoon of wind
ambled the oak trees   and arching aspens.

In happy half-sleep   I heard or half-heard
in the bliss of breeze   breath of my grandfather,
vaunt of his voice   advance us vaward.
No fears fretted me   and a freedom followed
this vision vouchsafed,   victory of spirit.
He in the wind   wept not, but wonderfully
spoke softly   soothing to peace.

What mattered he murmured   I never remembered,
words melted in wisps   washed whitely away;
but calm came into me   and cool repose.
Where Fate had fixed   no fervor formed;
he had accepted   wholeness of his handiwork.

gain it was given   to the Grace-grain that grew it,
had gone again   gleaming to Genesis

to the stark beginning   where the first stars burned.
Touchless and tristless   Time took it anew
and changed that church-plot   to an enchanted chrisom
of leaf and flower   of lithe light and shade.

Pilgrim, the past   becomes prayer
becomes remembrance rock-real   of Resurrection
when the Willer so willeth   works his wild wonders.

                                        —Fred Chappell

5 🖋 Nonspecific Forms and Formal Elements

ENVELOPE VERSE. Any stanza or poem beginning and ending with the same line (see also Envelope in Glossary).

> Lo, what it is to love!
> Lerne ye that list to prove
>   At me, I say,
>   No ways that may
> The ground of grieff remove
>   My liff alweie
>   That doeth decaye:
> Lo, what it is to love!
>
> —Sir Thomas Wyatt

SHELLEY

> Each had her claim.
> To each he gave consent:
> To water, his liquid name,
> His burning body to flame,
> To earth the sediment
> And the snatched heart, his fame
> To the four winds. He went
> As severally as he came—
> Element to element.
> Each had her claim.
>
> —Robert Francis

MIRROR IMAGE. Any poem in which conjoining prosodic elements are reversed. In the first example, the line lengths (by number of stresses or feet) alternate by stanza between five, four, three, three,

four, five, and three, four, five, five, four, three; the rhyme pattern for
each stanza is abccba, which is also the rhyme scheme by which the
TERCETS mirror each other in the second poem.

LIMITS

FLORIDA FROGMEN FIND NEW WORLD
 — *The New York Times*

Within the limestone mantle of the shelf
  Beneath the swamp, the cypress root,
    The great resort hotels
    Of Florida, other hells
  Are trespassed by the webbed foot
Beating to print the water's self with self.

    Leaching the whole of truth
  Ruined heroes of the daily mind,
Those undergoing scholars climb upstream
Into a darkness prior to their dream,
  Where the dividing eye is blind.
    Therein they spend their youth.

Inside the pouched, hard hide of the riddled earth
  They flutter, determined frogmen, ready
    To carry air and light
    Into the condemned, tight
  Tenements of the old landlady
Till she have rent them more than bed and birth.

    Under the rib, inside,
  Air gone, and battery burned out,
Is there a second, till the lungs have burst,
Of a second freedom, greater than the first,
  When the young frog prince, born of doubt,
    Swims down upon his bride?

She drags him to her as a mirror would
  Now shrieking Oedipus is blind
    And fair Narcissus cold,
    The dragon-guarded gold,

All that was lost, they fall to find,
Losing their science, which is understood.

—Howard Nemerov

LADY IN WAITING

She would be there waiting, so they said,
eager for him, his body toned by flight,
his head full of cossack horses rearing.

Instead he found seamy strangers scheming
how to make the tight thighed lady right.
They rushed the blood-shot immigrant to bed.

Once there he had to do it all alone,
mouth to mouth resuscitate the drowned,
soothe her pale bones, her too blue lips,

kiss those delicate ears, fondle the tips
of her most intricate designs. Gowned
in a scarlet peignoir, at last she made sweet moan.

They lay there in a soothing afterglow
until the lady rose, dimly crossed the room,
pushed his window up, then laughed and laughed.

He shivered in the unexpected draft,
felt all her colors fading into gloom,
love squelched and nowhere else to go.

She slit his pockets, dismembered both his shoes,
with a grotesque giggle kicked his underwear
into the shadows underneath the bed.

It took a while to drive her from his head,
to munch his roll, say he didn't care
she'd left him naked with nothing more to lose.

—Dan Jaffe

TENZONE. Origin uncertain, despite the Italian name. Most highly developed in Italy and in twelfth-century Provence. Popularized by

Giacomo da Leutino, Jacopo Mostacci, and Guittone d'Grezzo, the form is defined only as an argument in formal verse, usually between abstract qualities, such as the Body and the Soul in the following example, entitled "Tenzone."

SOUL TO BODY

That affable, vital, inspired even, and well-paid
    persuader of sensibility with the witty asides
but, at core, lucent and unswayed—
    a gem of serenest ray—besides
    being the well-known poet, critic, editor, and middle-high
    aesthete of the circuit is, alas, I.

Some weep for him: a waster of talent. Some
    snicker at the thought of talent in him. He leaves
in a Cadillac, has his home away from home
    where the dolls are, and likes it. What weaves
    vine leaves in the hair weaves no laurel for the head.
    The greedy pig, he might as well be dead—

to art at least—for wanting it all and more—
    cash, bourbon, his whim away from whom.
He's a belly, a wallet, a suit, a no-score
    of the soul. Sure, he looks like a boom
    coming, but whatever he comes to, sits to, tries
    to sit still to and say, is a bust. It's booby prize

time at the last dance whenever he
    lets a silence into himself. It grinds
against the jitter in him and dies. Poetry
    is what he grabs at, then dabbles in when he finds
    hobby time for it between serious pitches
    for cash, free-loading, and the more expensive bitches.

I give him up, say I. (And so say I.)
    There are no tears in him. If he does feel,
he's busier at Chateaubriand than at asking why.
    He lives the way he lives as if it were real.
    A con man. A half truth. A swindler in the clear.
    Look at him guzzle. He actually likes it here!

BODY TO SOUL

That grave, secretive, aspirant even, and bang-kneed
    eternalist of boneyards with the swallowed tongue
but, at dream source, flaming and fire-freed—
    a monk of dark-celled rays—along
    with being heretic, ignorant, Jesuit, and who-
    knows-what skeleton, is, alas, not wholly you.

I've watched you: a scratcher of scabs that are not
    there. An ectoplasmic jitter. Who was it spent
those twenty years and more in the polyglot
    of nightmares talking to Pa? If I went
    over your head to God, it *was* over your head.
    Whose butt grew stiff in the chair the nights you read

whose eyes blind and wrote whose nerves to a dither?
    And who got up in the cold to revise you by light?
You're a glowworm. A spook. A half-strung zither
    with a warped sounding box: you plunk all right
    but if what whines out is music, an alley cat
    in moon-heat on a trashcan is Kirsten Flagstadt.

Yes, I like it here. Make it twenty times worse
    and I'd still do it over again, even with you
like a monkey on my back. You dried-out wet-nurse,
    think you're the poet, do you? You're wind that blew
    on ashes that wouldn't catch. You were gone
    the instant I learned the poem is belly and bone.

I gave *you* up. Like a burp. For a better weather
    inside my guts. And, *yes*, I want it all—
grab, gaggle, and rut—as sure as death's no breather.
    Though you wouldn't know, being dead as yesterday's squall
    where the sea's a diamond-spilling toss in the bright brace
    of today's air, to glitter me time and place.

                          —John Ciardi

ACROSTIC. An acrostic is any poem in which the first letters of the
lines, read down the page, spell out a message or a name. This is done
meaningfully only with rhymed and measured verse, since there is

clearly no challenge or accomplishment in putting the needed words in place at the beginnings of the lines if there is no stricture at the other end. A *double crostic* spells out something at each end of the lines, as for instance:

G . . . . .T
L . . . . .O
O . . . . .G
R . . . . .O
Y . . . . .D

ACROSTIC ON A LINE FROM TOM T. HALL

Softly the robin poked among the grass
Obeying April's golden ordinance
Mindless of why that skyblue ball of sass
Equally needed to leap down and pounce
To keep her at a decent distance from
Holier ground the jay was mistress of,
If only by the jay's own cognizance.
No matter what they called what they called home,
God was its daddy, and his name was Love.

Innocent beings in this vale of grief
Seem to go on about their daily wars
Gorgeously indisposed to one belief
Or other as to why this world of ours
Is all so bloody. Something's going to kill
Not one but all of us before too long.
Goodness may set the movements of the stars
To music humming in the primal chill.
Otherwise, mayhem does the countersong.

Keep this in mind if any merriment
Incline you to think joy comes out of pain.
Love is the jaybird's bickering descent.
Love is the robin hunting after rain.
Unsavory as it is, the murderous
So far outnumber everybody else

As to give evidence that the Big Plan
Leaves little likelihood the likes of us
Look forward to outlive the thing that kills.

—Michael Heffernan

SPATIALS AND CONCRETE POETRY. The spatial poem, or shaped poem, depends for much of its effect on its *visible* pattern. It is an ancient kind of verse. The traditional shapes, with now vague symbolic associations, are these:

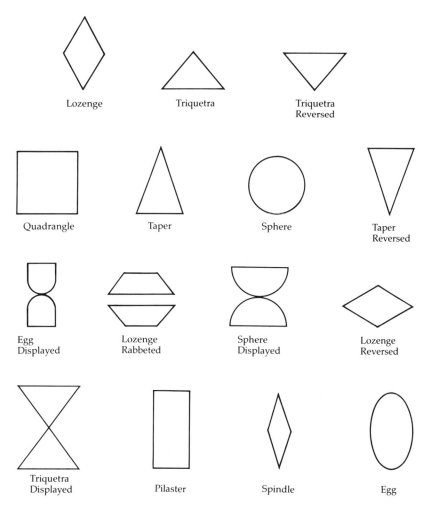

| Lozenge | Triquetra | Triquetra Reversed |

| Quadrangle | Taper | Sphere | Taper Reversed |

| Egg Displayed | Lozenge Rabbeted | Sphere Displayed | Lozenge Reversed |

| Triquetra Displayed | Pilaster | Spindle | Egg |

Few poets employ those shapes nowadays, if many ever did, though Dylan Thomas built his long "Vision and Prayer" on the lozenge and the triquetra displayed, shapes suggesting the relationship between heaven and earth. Most spatial poems are imitative of more clearly interpreted shapes, usually objects or actions we recognize at once. In any spatial poem, of course, the shape must reinforce the statement of the poem. The term *concrete poetry* is sometimes used to describe these works.

EASTER-WINGS

Lord, who createdst man in wealth and store,
Though foolishly he lost the same,
Decaying more and more,
Till he became
Most poore:
With thee
O let me rise
As larks, harmoniously,
And sing this day thy victories:
Then shall the fall further the flight in me.

My tender age in sorrow did beginne:
And still with sickness and shame
Thou didst so punish sinne,
That I become
Most thinne.
With thee
Let me combine
And feel this day thy victorie:
For, if I imp my wing on thine,
Afflication shall advance the flight in me.

—George Herbert

THE ALTAR

A broken A L T A R, Lord, thy servant reares,
Made of a heart, and cemented with teares:
  Whose parts are as thy hand did frame;
  No workmans tool hath touch'd the same.
     A   H E A R T alone,
     Is such a stone,
     As nothing but
     Thy pow'r doth cut.
     Wherefore each part
     Of my hard heart
     Meets in this frame,
     To praise thy Name:
  That, if I chance to hold my peace,
  These stones to praise thee may not cease.
Oh let thy blessed S A C R I F I C E be mine,
And sanctifie this A L T A R to be thine.
        —George Herbert

The term *concrete poetry* is sometimes also used to indicate a kind of spatial poetry in which the manipulation of the word on the page creates a picture of the noun, "acts out" the verb, or draws a larger picture of the action described in a poem, as in the following two examples.

BEAUCOUP BUTTERCUPS

and c o w c o w c o w
   o o   o o   o o
   w   w   w
  parsley parsley parsley

the way a
whole field looks
back at you

in Berkshire in
June
      —Jonathan Williams

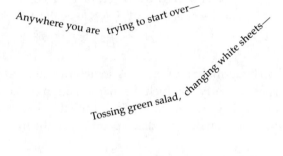

THE BLACK AND SMALL BIRDS OF REMORSE

come in the cool hours

one by one

to perch on the backs of chairs.

Anywhere you are trying to start over—

Tossing green salad, changing white sheets—

They glide in of a sudden,

shift from foot to foot

—Jo McDougall

QUANTITATIVE VERSE. Also referred to as *classical prosody*, from the Greek *prosodia*, the study and use of accent based on pitch. Since Latin times, the terms have been applied to the accenting of lines by the duration of syllables. Only roughly equivalent to the contemporary English "long" and "short" distinction, the difference is closer to that between "closed" and "open" vowels in Italian, where the designation depends more clearly (as in quantitative verse) upon the position of a vowel in relation to following consonants. Some length/position connection does exist in English—a vowel is usually long if it is followed by a consonant and an *e* (*file*) and short if it is followed by a double consonant (*fill*). But generally, English vowels are said to be long or short by their nature; that is to say, the difference is arbitrary and learned by rote.

Quantitative verse is not a designation for measure, such as a hexameter line, nor for a verse form, such as a sonnet; it is a *means* of measuring, comparable, say, to syllabics.

Briefly, the principles are these: A vowel is considered to be long if it is followed by two separate consonant sounds, even if the second begins a subsequent word; there are some exceptions, under which some vowels preceding single consonants may be long. A syllable is taken as long if it contains a vowel that is long by position or "by nature" (*i.e.*, diphthongs and English long vowels). Accent is of consequence; the long vowel plays the role that the accented syllable plays in English scansion. A spondee (indicated by the symbol −− rather than //) on an odd-numbered foot is accepted as an iamb in an iambic line.

The example below is a poem written in quantitative verse with the first stanza scanned. Here are the symbols used, and their meanings.

> ◡ = a short vowel
> = = a vowel long by nature (in English)
> — = a vowel long by position
> ◡̄ = a vowel that may be read long or short

Note that (as with syllabics) the measures in quantitative verse are not always (some would say not ever) clearly heard in English.

JOHANNES MILTON, SENEX

Sínce Ī|belíeve|in Gŏd|thĕ Fā|thĕr Āl|mĭghty,|
Mān's Mā|kĕr ănd|Jūdge, Ō|vĕrrū|lĕr ŏf|Fórtŭne,|

'Twere strange|should I|praise any|thing and|refuse|Him praise|
Should love|the crea|ture for|getting|the Cre|ator,|
Nor un|to Him|in suff|'ring and|sorrow|turn me:|
Nay how|could I|withdraw|me from|His em|bracing?|

But since that I have seen not, and cannot know Him,
Nor in my earthly temple apprehend rightly
His wisdom and the heav'nly purpose eternal;
Therefore will I be bound to no studied system
Nor argument, nor with delusion enslave me,
Nor seek to please Him in any foolish invention,
Which my spirit within me, that loveth beauty
And hateth evil, hath reprov'd as unworthy:

But I cherish my freedom in living service,
Gratefully adoring for delight beyond asking
Or thinking, and in hours of anguish and darkness
Confiding always on His excellent greatness.

—Robert Bridges

SYLLABIC VERSE. Syllabics, the measure of lines by syllable count rather than by stress on the metrical foot, is generally considered to be less effective in English than in French, a language without the patterns of stress we hear in English. Some English-language poets have employed syllabics with success, however; Marianne Moore made it her measure, Dylan Thomas used it, and Lewis Turco uses it extensively. For those forms originating in Welsh or French, syllabic measure is stipulated. Donald Justice has built the following fourteen-line poem on unrhymed lines of fourteen syllables each, with an effect akin to that of BLANK VERSE.

ON THE FARM

The boy, missing the city intensely at this moment,
Mopes and sulks at the window. There's the first owl now, quite near,
But the boy hardly notices. And the kerosene lamp
Yearns ceilingwards, giving off vague medicinal perfumes
That make him think of sickrooms. He has been memorizing
"The Ballad of Reading Gaol," but the lamplight hurts his eyes;

And he is too bored to sleep, restless and bored. *Years later,*
Perhaps, he will recall the evenings, empty and vast, when,
Under the first stars, there by the back gate, secretly, he
Had relieved himself on the shamed and drooping hollyhocks.
But now he yawns, and the old dream of being a changeling
Returns. And the owl cries, and the boy is like this owl—proud,
Almost invisible—or like the hero in Homer
Protected by a cloud let down by the gods to save him.

—Donald Justice

REPEATED TERMINAL WORDS AS A LINE-ENDING PATTERN.

The SESTINA is the only set form employing a pattern of terminal-word repetition, but any form may make use of it, as in the three poems below. In the second, word repetition changes to rhyme at the end as a closing device. The third and final example is a word-repetition SONNET.

GHOSTS

Some evenings, there are ghosts. There are. Ghosts
come in through the door when people come in,
being unable to open doors themselves
and not knowing (not knowing they are ghosts)

they could pass through anything, like thought.
They come and stand, move aimlessly about
as if each one of them had come to meet
someone who hadn't arrived. I always thought

of haunts and spirits as having a special power
like witches to do whatever they wanted to.
They don't. Pure energy without a cage
can do nothing at all. Whatever power

pushes or pulls the things of this world
to any purpose does it by piston or pistol,
mill-wheel or spring or some such pushing back.
Spirit freed fades into the world.

Inertia, which is habit, keeps their lines
a little while and then like memory

they weaken and fade. The glow is energy going.
They seem like actors trying to remember lines.

The trouble is they don't know they're dead.
We don't know very much about ghosts;
we think that some of those who weren't prepared
and died surprised don't understand they're dead

and hang around. The kindest thing to do
when you see one is simply to say
"Listen, you're dead. You're dead. Get out of here."
That's what the ghost eventually will do

when we've told it again and again to go.
"Get out of here. Get out of here. You're dead."
They can't of course go anywhere on purpose;
you have to give them intent to make them go.

And who knows where? All this has to do
with Newton's laws. The figure disappears.
Somewhere there's a place. Be kind. Be firm.
Remember the only thing you have to do

is tell them the truth. Say "You're dead. Get out."
Ignore the slow confusion on their faces.
Never pity. They can soak up pity.
Sympathy makes them denser and drags it out.

If pity comes, don't let it go to them.
Watch for a sudden change in temperature.
You still have a death to deal with.
Pity yourself, who could be one of them

to live—as it were—with all the embarrassment.
You would not want someone who sounds like
a movie director telling you you're dead.
Your tissue hands could not hide the embarrassment.

—Miller Williams

FOR THE LIFE OF HIM AND HER

For the life of her she couldn't decide what to wear to the party.
All those clothes in the closet and not a thing to wear.

Nothing to wear, nothing wearable to a party,
Nothing at all in the closet for a girl to wear.

For the life of him he couldn't imagine what she was doing up there.
She had been messing around in that closet for at least an hour,
Trying on this, trying on that, trying on all those clothes up there,
So that they were already late for the party by at least an hour.

If only he wouldn't stand around down in the hall,
She could get herself dressed for the party, she knew she could
    somehow,
But he made her so nervous, he was so nervous there in the hall
That she didn't think they would get to the party anyhow.

He didn't want to go to the party anyhow,
And he didn't want to stand and stand in the hall,
But he didn't want to tell her he didn't want to go anyhow.
He just didn't want to, that's all.

—Reed Whittemore

THE ILLITERATE

Touching your goodness, I am like a man
Who turns a letter over in his hand
And you might think this was because the hand
Was unfamiliar but, truth is, the man
Has never had a letter from anyone;
And now he is both afraid of what it means
And ashamed because he has no other means
To find out what it says than to ask someone.

His uncle could have left the farm to him,
Or his parents died before he sent them word,
Or the dark girl changed and want him for beloved.
Afraid and letter-proud, he keeps it with him.
What would you call his feeling for the words
That keep him rich and orphaned and beloved?

—William Meredith

6 ✑ Variations on the Stanzas

SPLIT COUPLET VARIATION

THE PYTHON

Glassed in
what is, if not chagrin,

despair
he blunts the fetid air

the zoo
contains and scarcely moves.

He'd seem
a root, our sourest dream

with eyes
that one hates in surprise.

How few
the things he lives to do.

How wise,
elaborate his guise.

—Gordon Osing

LONG HYMNAL MEASURE VARIATION. This is in effect a curtal
LONG HYMNAL MEASURE; *i.e.*, the last line of that pattern is cut short.
(The example that follows happens to be an *Horatian ode*, which is not
a set pattern; any poem of any number of formal stanzas may be given
the name.)

AN HORATIAN ODE TO THE KING'S MOST EXCELLENT MAJESTY
(22ND JUNE, 1911)

Not with high-vaulting phrase, or rush
   Of weak-winged epithets that tire
With their own weight, or formal gush,
     We greet thee, Sire!

To flights less lofty we aspire.
   We pray, in speech unskilled to feign,
That all good things good men desire
     May crown Thy reign;

That our State "Dreadnought" once again
   May leave in broken seas to veer,
And shape her course direct and plain,
     With Thee to steer,

Into blue sky and water clear,
   Where she on even keel shall ride,
Secure from reef and shoal, or fear
     Of wind and tide.

So may it be, Sire!—so abide!
   Till, by God's grace, this Empire shine
More great in power than great in pride,
     Through Thee and Thine;

Nor from her honoured past resign
   One least bequest; or vail her claim
To aught that dowers an ancient line—
     An ancient fame!

                 —Austin Dobson

SPENSERIAN VARIATION. Howard Nemerov has combined distinctive elements of two forms in the poem below to build what can fairly be called a Spenserian quintilla.

THE SECOND-BEST BED

Consider now that Troy has burned
—Priam is dead, and Hector dead,

And great Aeneas long since turned
Away seaward with his gods
To find, found or founder, against frightful odds.

And figure to yourselves the clown
Who comes with educated word
To illustrate in mask and gown
King Priam's most illustrious son
And figure forth his figure with many another one

Of that most ceremented time
In times have been or are to be
Inhearsed in military rime;
And will recite of royal fates
Until, infamonized among those potentates

By a messenger from nearer home,
His comedy is compromised
And he must leave both Greece and Rome
Abuilding but not half begun,
To play the honest Troyan to a girl far gone.

The wench lived on, if the son died—
All Denmark wounded in one bed
Cried vengeance on the lusty bride,
Who could not care that there would follow,
After the words of Mercury, songs of Apollo.

—Howard Nemerov

HEROIC SESTET VARIATION. The HEROIC SESTET is made of a heroic quatrain and a HEROIC COUPLET. Here an ITALIAN QUATRAIN is joined to the couplet.

THE HUMAN CONDITION

In this motel where I was told to wait,
The television screen is stood before
The picture window. Nothing could be more
Use to a man than knowing where he's at,
And I don't know, but pace the day in doubt
Between my looking in and looking out.

Through snow, along the snowy road, cars pass
Going both ways, and pass behind the screen
Where heads of heroes sometimes can be seen
And sometimes cars, that speed across the glass.
Once I saw world and thought exactly meet,
But only in a picture by Magritte.

A picture of a picture, by Magritte,
Wherein a landscape on an easel stands
Before a window opening on a land-
scape, and the pair of them a perfect fit,
Silent and mad. You know right off, the room
Before that scene was always an empty room.

And that is now the room in which I stand
Waiting, or walk, and sometimes try to sleep.
The day falls into darkness while I keep
The TV going; headlights blaze behind
Its legendary traffic, love and hate,
In this motel where I was told to wait.

—Howard Nemerov

In the following poem John Ciardi shortens each heroic-sestet line by one foot. It is in effect a *short heroic sestet*, a term with a strong oxymoronic suggestion.

TALKING MYSELF TO SLEEP AT ONE MORE HILTON

I have a country but no town.
Home ran away from me. My trees
ripped up their white roots and lay down.
Bulldozers cut my lawn. All these
are data toward some sentiment
like money: God knows where it went.

There was a house as sure as time.
Sure as my father's name and grave.
Sure as trees for me to climb.
Sure as behave and misbehave.
Sure as lamb stew. Sure as sin.
As warts. As games. As a scraped shin.

There was a house, a chicken run,
a garden, guilt, a rocking chair.
I had six dogs and every one
was killed in traffic. I knew where
their bones were once. Now I'm not sure.
Roses used them for manure.

There was a house early and late.
One day there came an overpass.
It snatched the stew right off my plate.
It snatched the plate. A whiff of gas
blew up the house like a freak wind.
I wonder if I really mind.

My father died. My father's house
fell out of any real estate.
My dogs lie buried where time was
when time still flowed, where now a slate
stiff river loops, called Exit Nine.
Why should I mind? It isn't mine.

I have the way I think I live.
The doors of my expense account
open like arms when I arrive.
There is no cloud I cannot mount
and sip good bourbon as I ride.
My father's house is Hilton-wide.

What are old dog bones? Were my trees
still standing would I really care?
What's the right name for this disease
of wishing they might still be there
if I went back, though I will not
and never meant to?—Smash the pot,

knock in the windows, blow the doors.
I am not and mean not to be
what I was once. I have two shores
five hours apart, soon to be three.
And home is anywhere between.
Sure as the airport limousine,

sure as credit, sure as a drink,
as the best steak you ever had,
as thinking—when there's time to think—
it's good enough. At least not bad.
Better than dog bones and lamb stew.
It does. Or it will have to do.

—John Ciardi

7 🦋 Variations on the Poems

RIME ROYAL VARIATION

THE PRIVATE EYE

To see clearly, not to be deceived
By the pretended burial of the dead,
    The tears of the bereaved,
    The stopped clock
    Or impenetrable lock,
Or anything that possibly was said
Simply to see who might have been misled;

To dig down deep enough to find the truth,
To penetrate and check, balance and sift,
    Pretending to be uncouth
    And a little dumb
    Till the truth come,
Till the proud and wicked give away their drift
Out of security—that is my gift,

To seem omnivorous in my belief,
Ready to swallow anything at first,
    (Knowing the corrupt chief
    Had rigged the raid
    So no arrest was made)
And, acting guileless as an infant nursed,
Believe in nothing till I get the worst.

I know what cannot possibly be known,
And never know I know it till the end.
    When justice must be done

I give the word
To the honestly bored
Survivors of my lust to apprehend,
And then, with the bourbon and the blonde, unbend.

　　　　　　　　　　　—Howard Nemerov

SONNET VARIATIONS. Most sonnet variations are untraditional only in the rhyme schemes, which avoid the Italian, English, and Spenserian stanzas alike.

SONNET AT EASTER

You splice together two broomsticks, then reef
A tie (a Christmas present) at the throat.
A hat must rattle on the knob, a coat
Keep warm the chest (for he has little beef).
You set this person up disguised as you
And let him flap. He hangs lonely as grief.
His wraithless hull, no blood and no belief,
Your children don't despise but your crows do.

He is a habit now, perennial,
One of your pieties. You plant him deep,
And though you have no earthly use for him
You dress him in your father's coat, and call
Good Evening sometimes when the light is dim,
Seeing he stands for you in upright sleep.

　　　　　　　　　　　—Howard Nemerov

Many sonnet variations combine the Italian and English rhyme schemes, as does the following poem.

THE RURAL CARRIER STOPS TO KILL A NINE-FOOT COTTONMOUTH

Lord God, I saw the son-of-a-bitch uncoil
In the road ahead of me, uncoil and squirm
For the ditch, squirm a hell of a long time.
Missed him with the car. When I got back to him, he was all
But gone, nothing left on the road but the tip-end

Of his tail, and that disappearing into Johnson grass.
I leaned over the ditch and saw him, balled up now, hiss.
I aimed for the mouth and shot him. And shot him again.

Then I got a good strong stick and dragged him out.
He was long and evil, thick as the top of my arm.
There are things in this world a man can't look at without
Wanting to kill. Don't ask me why. I was calm
Enough, I thought. But I felt my spine
Squirm suddenly. I admit it. It was mine.

                                                              —T. R. Hummer

   Donald Justice creates highly conversational variations on the sonnet form in the following two poems. He also shifts the rhetorical patterns, with the resolving moves taking place in the final five lines in
the first and the final three and one-third lines in the second; this
opens an opportunity there for an additional rhyme that is both inte-
rior and terminal in effect. Note in the second line of "At the Cemetery" the insertion of a *rest* (to borrow a term from music) to serve as a
silent beat.

ON THE PORCH

There used to be a way the sunlight caught
The caterpillar webs in the pecans.
The boy's shadow would lengthen to a man's
Across the grass then, slowly. And if he thought
Some sleepy god had dreamed it all up—well,
There stood the grandfather, Lincoln-tall and solemn,
Tapping his pipe against the white-flaked column,
Carefully, carefully, as though it were his job;
And they would watch the pipe-stars as they fell.
As for the stillness, the same train always broke it,
At which the great gold watch rose from its pocket
And they would check the hour—the dark fob
Dangling the watch between them like a moon.
It would be evening soon then, very soon.

                                                              —Donald Justice

AT THE CEMETERY

But why do I write of the all unutterable and the all abysmal?
Why does my pen not drop from my hand on approaching
the infinite pity and tragedy of all the past?
It does, poor helpless pen, with what it meets of the ineffable,
what it meets of the cold Medusa-face of life, of all the life
lived, on every side. *Basta, Basta!* —Henry James, *Notebooks*

Above the fence-flowers, like a bloody thumb,
A hummingbird was throbbing . . . Some
Petals too motion then from the beaten wings
In hardly observable obscure quiverings.
And the mother stood there, but so still her clothing
Seemed to be turning into stone, nothing to see there
But the monotonous sculpturings of the weather.
She stood this way for a long time while the sky
Pondered her with its great Medusa-eye;
Or in the boy's memory she did.
                              And then a
Slow blacksnake, lazy with long sunning, slid
Down from its slab, and through the thick grass, and hid
Somewhere among the purpling wild verbena.

                                        —Donald Justice

In the next sonnet variation Dave Smith's slant rhyme locks the almost Shakespearean final two lines back to the third quatrain.

A MAN'S DAUGHTER

From the hill's high crown, it looked like a plane of grass
but this was light's trick, and thick as nightmare, the plunge
of wind and shadow disguising the lake. She told me how last
week she'd thought the calendar's red X was wrong, and lunged

ahead, blithe on that dangerous ground. The algae lay dark in drifts
under clear water. Slowly the light changed upward and the black
of storm shrank around that place. We stood like birds against wind
ripping the silver of water. Rain beat at our faces and backs.

The few words we had, we spoke and left. Somewhere we heard
    trunks

bending and keening. Then stillness. Then sky went gold and her face
sang up for a circling loon. I am a man with a man's good luck.
I saw her kneel for the tender crop at the black place.

I watched the water clear, watched her glitter. How green all was,
and overhead a bird's white belly wheeled like a moon for love.

—Dave Smith

The following unrhymed sonnet earns the name not only because of
its fourteen lines of iambic pentameter, but also because its structure
otherwise is that of the sonnet; the description of a circumstance (in
an octave, usually) and a resolving comment on it (usually in a sestet).

THE REMORSE FOR TIME

When I was a boy, I used to go to bed
By daylight, in the summer, and lie awake
Between the cool, white, reconciling sheets,
Hearing the talk of birds, watching the light
Diminish through the shimmering planes of leaf
Outside the window, until sleep came down
When darkness did, eyes closing as the light
Faded out of them, silencing the birds.

Sometimes still, in the sleepless dark hours
Tormented most by the remorse for time,
Only for time, the mind speaks of that boy
(He did no wrong, then why had he to die?)
Falling asleep on the current of the stars
Which even then washed him away past pardon.

—Howard Nemerov

Fourteen words have rarely done such duty as in the following sonnet, which differs from the traditional form only in not having ten
syllables per line and in the combining of the Italian octave and the
Shakespearean sestet.

AN AERONAUT TO HIS LOVE

I
Through
Blue
Sky
Fly
To
You.
Why?
Sweet
Love,
Feet
Move
So
Slow.
   —Witter Bynner

In the final example the SESTINA is a strong presence in the sonnet, or the sonnet in the sestina, as the two forms seem equally present.

A COLLOQUY OF SILENCES

That calm above those trees in the gray spaces
among the crosswork of the twigs and branches
and thin birdwhistle piping into silence
with other further birds whistling in answer
among the selfsame silences. I answer:
we weren't meant to live among these spaces
except to scare our hearts out in the silence
that makes us wonder what the upper branches
of trees can have learned about the main branches
of wisdom and the sources of the answer
to the question about why all this silence
must persist among those elegant spaces
beyond the gray spaces around tree branches
where the silences of birds are the answer.
                    —Michael Heffernan

RONDEAU VARIATIONS

RONDEAU

Jenny kissed me when we met,
　Jumping from the chair she sat in;
Time, you thief, who love to get
　Sweets into your list, put that in:
Say I'm weary, say I'm sad,
　Say that health and wealth have missed me.
Say I'm growing old, but add,
　Jenny kissed me.

　　　　　　　　　　　—Leigh Hunt

ASK ME NO MORE

Ask me no more: the moon may draw the sea;
　The cloud may stoop from heaven and take the shape,
　With fold to fold, of mountain or cape;
But O too fond, when have I answered thee?
　　　　　Ask me no more.

Ask me no more: what answer should I give?
　I love not hollow cheek or faded eye:
　Yet, O my friend, I will not have thee die!
Ask me no more, lest I should bid thee live;
　　　　　Ask me no more.

Ask me no more: thy fate and mine are sealed;
　I strove against the stream and all in vain;
　Let the great river take me to the main.
No more, dear love, for at a touch I yield;
　　　　　Ask me no more.

　　　　　　　　　　—Alfred, Lord Tennyson

SESTINA VARIATIONS. Probably no form lends itself so interest-
ingly to experiment as does the sestina. The following one uses the
words of the first line (excepting the pronouns) as the repeated words,
and closes on a single line instead of the traditional three. All of the

first lines and the last line use the same words in different syntactical orders (with a variation in stanza 2).

THE OBSESSION

Last night I dreamed my father died again,
a decade and a year after he dreamed
of death himself, pitched forward into night.
His world of waking flickered out and died—
an image on a screen. He is the father
now of fitful dreams that last and last.

I dreamed again my father died at last.
He stood before me in his flesh again.
I greeted him. I said, "How are you, father?"
But he looked frailer than last time I'd dreamed
we were together, older than when he'd died—
I saw upon his face the look of night.

I dreamed my father died again last night.
He stood before a mirror. He looked his last
into the glass and kissed it. He saw he'd died.
I put my arms around him once again
to help support him as he fell. I dreamed
I held the final heartburst of my father.

I died again last night: I dreamed my father
kissed himself in glass, kissed me goodnight
in doing so. But what was it I dreamed
in fact? An injury that seems to last
without abatement, opening again
and yet again in dream? Who was it died

again last night? I dreamed my father died,
but it was not he—it was not my father,
only an image flickering again
upon the screen of dream out of the night.
How long can this cold image of him last?
Whose is it, his or mine? Who dreams he dreamed?

My father died. Again last night I dreamed
I felt his struggling heart still as he died
beneath my failing hands. And when at last
he weighed me down, then I laid down my father,
covered him with silence and with night.
I could not bear it should he come again—

I died again last night, my father dreamed.

—Wesli Court

Here is an intricately diminishing sestina variation in which the traditional end-word permutation is replaced by a pattern of repetition of the end words in the same order (except for a reversal of two words at the second repetition) with each end word then disappearing in the following sequence:

End words 1 and 6 disappear in the first repetition of all words
End word 5 disappears in the second repetition
End word 4 in the third
End word 2 in the fourth
End word 3 in the fifth

In addition, each word is replaced in its last "appearance" by a word that rhymes with it.

End word 1	1 rhyme				
2	2	3	3	3	3 rhyme
3	3	2	2	2 rhyme	
4	4	4	4 rhyme		
5	5	5 rhyme			
6	6 rhyme				

THE CANNON BALL

Flash floods at dawn, rivers red with clay;
By noon a cracking sun, wind rasping my bones.
Behind me Gettysburg, the black muskets
Splintered, Brother James stiffened by rumor,
His only grave in my unsodded mind.

I carry death inside my saddlebags;
Its heaviness thumps the flanks of my sweating bay;
I feel its iron roughness in my bones.
We rode together, Brother, stalwart as muskets,
Ready as boys tracking a lusty rumor
Through the tall grass. Oh, what fool's gold we mined,
Wrapped in the glitter of spring! Our bravest flags
Rot now in the fields of Gettysburg where muskets
Rust beside the helter-skelter bones
Wrenched from their springs, and I hear a bodiless rumor
Walking the groves, whimpering like the wind.
My legs are stiff in the stirrups as twin muskets,
For I carry you in the litter of my bones,
James, the cannon ball pressing my side like a tumor.
But I will plant it soon, at sundown salute it with muskets,
A new grave in a land without old stones.
And if a dark truth grows, these hands will husk it.

                                               —Dan Jaffe

The trenta-sei, invented by John Ciardi, is a poem of six six-line stanzas, in which each line of the first stanza takes its turn in order as the opening line of a stanza. Like the SESTINA, it is a strong pattern not likely to get lost in the language of the poem. It seems less "thought about" than the sestina does, though, and certainly less than the VIL-LANELLE, the sense of which is also evoked by the rotating repetition of the opening lines. The five-stress accentual lines are rhymed as in a HEROIC SESTET: *ababcc*. The word *psilanthropic* in line 4 is a playful invention of Ciardi's that means "merely human." It comes from the Greek *psilos* (mere) and *anthropos* (generic man).

A TRENTA-SEI OF THE PLEASURE WE TAKE IN THE EARLY DEATH OF KEATS

It is old school custom to pretend to be sad
when we think about the early death of Keats.
The species-truth of the matter is we are glad.
Psilanthropic among exegetes,
I am so moved that when the plate comes by
I almost think to pay the God—but why?

When we think about the early death of Keats
we are glad to be spared the bother of dying ourselves.
His poems are a candy store of bitter-sweets.
We munch whole flights of angels from his shelves
drooling a sticky glut, almost enough
to sicken us. But what delicious stuff!

The species-truth of the matter is we are glad
to have a death to munch on. Truth to tell,
we are also glad to pretend it makes us sad.
When it comes to dying, Keats did it so well
we thrill to the performance. Safely here,
this side of the fallen curtain, we stand and cheer.

Psilanthropic among exegetes,
as once in a miles-high turret spitting flame,
I watched boys flower through orange winding sheets
and shammed a mourning because it put a name
to a death I might have taken—which in a way
made me immortal for another day.

I was so moved that when the plate came by
I had my dollar in hand to give to death
but changed to a penny—enough for the old guy,
and almost enough saved to sweeten my breath
with a toast I will pledge to the Ape of the Divine
in thanks for every death that spares me mine.

I almost thought of paying the God—but why?
Had the boy lived, he might have grown as dull
as Tennyson. Far better, I say, to die
and leave us a formed feeling. O beautiful,
pale, dying poet, fading as soft as rhyme,
the saddest music keeps the sweetest time.

—John Ciardi

The following sestina variation shows the (sometimes very attractive)
effects of the softening of forms that marks much contemporary verse,
as the repeated end words change from singular to plural and back,
and their closing order is

```
3 _____ 1
none _____ 6
5,4 _____ 2
```

with only one of the words in line 2 and three in line 3.

NIGHTSONG: FERRIS WHEEL BY THE SEA

Please don't call it a ladder of circles
driven by a broken wind from the sea.
Yes, I know the wind scrapes at the wheel
all night long, and that the waves claw at the ships,
and that the tide under our feet is relentless.
I know you know the true motion of stillness

but don't we descend into that stillness
only to rise again? Because it is not the wheel
but the viciousness of turning, the relentless
climb into the sky climbing in circles
like squirrels quarreling in a feeder, or ships
leaving the dock but never setting out to sea

that disturbs and compels us. It is not the sea
with its quarries of weeds and its quarrelsome ships
roaring as it pleases into the stillness
of its own blank voice, its own relentless
weaving and unweaving a confusing surface of circles,
a tiresome system of echoes. A buzzard that wheels

past the shimmering wood of the ferris wheel
frightens us into a momentary silence; its relentless
wings slice and flatten as it hovers in circles
over a shallow wreckage swinging in the sea
while we continue moving into our own stillness
first toward and then away from the stunned ship

now quartered under the surf. The ship
we ride in is a cage of steel circles
encircled by the fleck and moaning of the sea.
We try to speak, but the stillness

is deafening, words fall behind us, and the wheel
lifts into the sky. Besides, the sea is a relentless

mother, and like the wind she seems to relent less
and less as the night wears into a deeper stillness.
We watch the buzzard revolving over the ruined ship
like a descending plane or a horizontal wheel
rotating toward the kill. And still the sea
keeps turning and turning in a nightmare of blank circles.

We descend. The wheel continues its stupid circle
into the sky, but we are moving into a new stillness
relentless as the black ships setting out to sea.

—Edward Hirsch

TERZA RIMA VARIATIONS. Both of the following variations drop the interlocking middle rhyme in each TERCET, but they are resolved in different ways.

POTTER, VIDALIA

Vidalia Potter (who often as not
put sheet to show and quilt underneath
when she made the bed and always forgot

the social worker woman's name
and made coffee that went to waste
everytime the woman came,

who fretted about a festering sore
on one of the legs of one of the girls
and walked at six to the Safeway store

for bottle drinks—Dr. Pepper,
Strawberry Creme, a 7 Up—
bread and sliced bologna for supper,

who never was sick and never was well,
whose man had a job at the chicken plant
and told time by the quitting bell,

who loved her children as best she could
and washed the leg and swept the floor
sometimes and thought about the good

strong-smelling man who called her to bed
when he wasn't drunk and he wasn't tired)
never could get it fixed in her head
what the social worker said.

—Miller Williams

A DREAM NEAR WATER
for John Engels

You walk toward the river. White flecks in your beard have gone;
But so has the beard. Completely. You're surprised,
Bending to cup up water, at the glossy tone

Of your skin. You notice too the wave and swell
Of your arms. All the women—girls, really—
You have ever known: they seem to be wishing you well

From the opposite leafy bank. As one, they stand
In smiles, wearing the billowy loose beach suits
Of another time, breeze-ruffled, extending their hands.

It's before the invention of clocks, or any chronometer.
(Amazing, what this means to time in the dream.)
So save your distinctions—*happy, sad*—for later.

For you feel no desire. You'll recall a pleasant view
And directly, the taste of water so clean you'll ache,
But not until awake, with something like sorrow.

Slim birds are fluting from the clickety reeds,
Pastels. Your children aren't a factor. Summer
Looms, as wide as ocean. This soft morning haze

Will be half the day burning off, uncountable hours
Will pass before your father sends up to your window,
Through which the dusk air puffs a scent of flowers,

His familiar whistle of greeting. He's come home
From a day trip on the lake. Later, he'll mount
The stairs to tuck you away in the violet room

Where, for a time that passes slow as an age,
You attend to tales that provoke unthinking laughter,
To your mother whose sobs are beading like dew on the page,

To the June frogs that wake and call to you over calm water.

                                                —Sydney Lea

BLANK VERSE VARIATIONS. The following poem, in octosyllabic, four-stress, unrhymed lines, is short-line blank verse. Because of the large number of foot variations, the accentual-syllabic nature of the lines tends to be lost in the reading and only the accentual element is heard. This is characteristic of the octosyllabic, four-stress line.

TRADITIONAL RED

Returning after dark, I thought,
The house will have grown small: noises
In the barn I knew, wood and field,
All tree tops visible. My eyes,
I thought, lied then or will lie now;
My ears, even my ears, will tell
Me: small. Then half awake I waited,
Half afraid of the sound light makes
With frost on the windowpanes. But night
Birds carried fifteen years away
Like an abandoned nest, put them
To rest somewhere I couldn't see
Without undoing anything,
And when I woke the dawn I saw
Was on the farm as positive as God.

A rooster dipped in sunlight raised
His crown, called to the steaming barn,
Gigantic, red, until my blood
Roared for stupidity, and I

Ran down the path humble with hens
To kneel and stare dumb wonder
At his size. My pride! my pride! O
Jesus, bright dove call! I knelt there
In his thunder, white and small, watched
Him and rose to walk under trees
Whose tops I couldn't see for light,
Dense, golden, moving hosts of leaves
Answering that red cry. And when
I turned I saw the farm house roof
Raking an iron rooster through the sky.

—Robert Huff

John Ciardi has built a blank verse poem with five-stress accentual lines each of which is complete in sense and syntax.

WASHING YOUR FEET

Washing your feet is hard when you get fat.

* * *

In lither times the act was unstrained and pleasurable.

* * *

You spread the toes for signs of athlete's foot.

* * *

You used creams, and rubbing alcohol, and you powdered.

* * *

You bent over, all in order, and did everything.

* * *

Mary Magdalene made a prayer meeting of it.

* * *

She, of course, was washing not her feet but God's.

* * *

Degas painted ladies washing their own feet.

* * *

Somehow they also seem to be washing God's feet.

*   *   *

To touch any body anywhere should be ritual.

*   *   *

To touch one's own body anywhere should be ritual.

*   *   *

Fat makes the ritual wheezy and a bit ridiculous.

*   *   *

Ritual and its idea should breathe easy.

*   *   *

They are memorial, meditative, immortal.

*   *   *

Toenails keep growing after one is dead.

*   *   *

Washing my feet, I think of immortal toenails.

*   *   *

What are they doing on these ten crimped polyps?

*   *   *

I reach to wash them and begin to wheeze.

*   *   *

I wish I could paint like Degas or believe like Mary.

*   *   *

It is sad to be naked and to lack talent.

*   *   *

It is sad to be fat and to have dirty feet.

—John Ciardi

Appendix A: Additional Poems in the Various Patterns

Note: Sources of the poems listed are cited only in the case of contemporary works. Older poems are easily located in standard anthologies.

BALLAD STANZA

Anonymous. "The Wife of Usher's Well."

BALLADE

Austin Dobson. "A Ballade to Queen Elizabeth."
William Ernest Henley. "Ballade of Youth and Age."
Barbara Howes. "Ballade of the Inventory: In Provence." In *Light and Dark*. Middletown, Conn., 1959.
Richard Wilbur. "Ballade for the Duke of Orleans." In *Poems of Richard Wilbur*. New York, 1963.

BLANK VERSE

Richard Wilbur. "Digging for China." In *Poems of Richard Wilbur*. New York, 1963.
W. S. Merwin. "The Fishermen." In *Green with Beasts*. New York, 1956.

CHANT ROYAL

Lewis Turco. "The Old Professor." In *First Poems*. Colton, Calif., 1960.

COMMON MEASURE

Emily Dickinson. "We never know how high we are . . ."

COUPLET, HEROIC

Miller Williams. "Leaving New York on the Penn Central to Metuchen." In *Halfway from Hoxie*. Baton Rouge, 1977.

COUPLET, SHORT

Miller Williams. "Thinking Friday Night with a Gothic Storm Going . . ." In *Halfway from Hoxie*. Baton Rouge, 1977.

COUPLET, SPLIT

J. V. Cunningham. "I, Too, Have Been to the Huntington." In *The Collected Poems and Epigrams of J. V. Cunningham*. Chicago, 1971.
Lewis Turco. "Lafe Grat." In *Pocoangelini*. Northampton, Mass., 1971.
Miller Williams. "Getting Experience." In *Why God Permits Evil*. Baton Rouge, 1981.

DOUBLE DACTYL

Anthony Harrington. *Tersery Versery*. Atlanta, 1982.
Anthony Hecht and John Hollander. *Jiggery Pokery: A Compendium of Double Dactyls*. New York, 1967.
Jim Harrison. *Outlyer and Ghazals*. New York, 1971.

HAIKU

William Howard, trans. In *To Walk in Seasons*. Rutland, Vt., 1972.
Lewis Turco. "Pentacles." In *Seasons of the Blood*. Rochester, 1980.

HEROIC SESTET

Karl Shapiro. "Waitress." In *Collected Poems*. New York, 1978.

HYMNAL MEASURE

Robert Herrick. "To the Virgins to Make Much of Time."
Langston Hughes. "Cross." In *Selected Poems*. New York, 1954.
John Suckling. "Song."

KYRIELLE

Phyllis McGinley. "Sunday Psalm." In *The Love Letters of Phyllis McGinley*. New York, 1954.

LIMERICK

Isaac Asimov and John Ciardi. *Limericks: Too Gross*. New York, 1978.
———. *A Grossery of Limericks*. New York, 1981.
William S. Baring-Gould, ed. *The Lure of the Limerick*. New York, 1967.

ODE, ENGLISH

John Keats. "Ode on a Grecian Urn."

ODE, HORATIAN

William Collins. "Horatian Ode."

QUINTILLA

Robert Frost. "The Road Not Taken." In *The Poetry of Robert Frost*. New York, 1969.

Karl Shapiro. "Epitaph for John and Richard." In *Collected Poems*. New York, 1978.

QUATRAIN, CURTAL

Archibald MacLeish. "Not Marble Nor the Gilded Monument." In *New and Collected Poems*. Boston, 1976.

QUATRAIN, HEROIC

Miller Williams. "All He Ever Wanted." In *Distractions*. Baton Rouge, 1981.

QUATRAIN, ITALIAN

John Crowe Ransom. "Vision by Sweetwater." In *Selected Poems*. New York, 1969.

QUATRAIN, SICILIAN

Richard Wilbur. "Mind." In *Poems of Richard Wilbur*. New York, 1963.

RONDEAU

W. H. Auden. "The Hidden Law." In *Collected Shorter Poems*. New York, 1964.
William Ernest Henley. "When You Are Old."
Barbara Howes. "Death of a Vermont Farm Woman." In *Light and Dark*. Middletown, Conn., 1959.

PANTOUM

Wesli Court. "The Eunuch Cat." In *Courses in Lambents*. Oswego, N.Y., 1977.

RONDEL

X. J. Kennedy. "Rondeau." In *Nude Descending a Staircase*. New York, 1951.

SESTET, HEROIC

John Ciardi. "To W. T. Scott." In *39 Poems*. New Brunswick, N.J., 1959.

SESTINA

W. H. Auden. "Paysage Moralise." In *Collected Shorter Poems*. New York, 1964.
Elizabeth Bishop. "Sestina." In *Collected Poems*. New York, 1973.

John Engels. "Sestina: My Dead in the First Show." In *Signals from the Safety Coffin*. Pittsburgh, 1975.
Robert Francis. "Hallelujah: A Sestina." In *Come Out into the Sun*. Amherst, Mass., 1965.
Donald Justice. "A Dream Sestina." In *Selected Poems*. New York, 1979.
Lewis Turco. "The Forest of My Seasons." In *Awaken, Bells Falling*. Columbia, Mo., 1968.

SKELTONICS

Lewis Turco. "Odds Bodkin's Strange Thrusts and Ravels." In *Poetry: An Introduction Through Writing*. Reston, Va., 1973.

SONNET, CAUDATE

John Milton. "On the New Forces of Conscience Under the Long Parliament."

SONNET, ITALIAN

Anthony Hecht. "Heureux qui, comme Ulysse, a fait un beau voyage." In *The Hard Hours*. New York, 1966.
John Keats. "On First Looking into Chapman's Homer."
William Wordsworth. "Sonnet (The world is too much with us . . .)."

SONNET, SHAKESPEAREAN

Howard Nemerov. "A Primer of the Daily Round." In *The Collected Poems of Howard Nemerov*. Chicago, 1977.

SPENSERIAN STANZA

Robert Bagg. "The Tandem Ride." In *Madonna of the Cello*. Middletown, Conn., 1961.
George Gordon, Lord Byron. "Childe Harold's Pilgrimage."
John Updike. "The Dance of the Solids." In *Midpoint and Other Poems*. New York, 1969.

TANKA

Lewis Turco. "Turn," "Cups," and "Judgment." In *Seasons of the Blood*. Rochester, 1980.

TERCET

John Ciardi. "The Colossus in Quicksand." In *Person to Person*. New Brunswick, N.J., 1964.

Theodore Roethke. "The Sloth." In *Collected Poems of Theodore Roethke*. New York, 1975.

TERZA RIMA

Thomas Hardy. "Starlings on the Roof."
Karl Shapiro. "Jew." In *Collected Poems*. New York, 1978.
Percy Bysshe Shelley. "Ode to the West Wind."

TRIOLET

Lewis Turco. "Jasper Olson." In *Pocoangelini*. Northampton, Mass., 1971.

VILLANELLE

Dylan Thomas. "Do Not Go Gentle into That Good Night." In *Collected Poems*. New York, 1952.

Appendix B: Some Applications of Certain Devices of Structural Linguistics to Prosody

Using the techniques of traditional scansion, we analyze the rhythms of a line of poetry by identifying and counting the metrical feet and noting imperfect and reversed feet as well as caesuras and the effect of all these on the placement and strength of accents. For instance, the first two lines of Roethke's "I Knew a Woman" might be scanned like this, with feet divided by single vertical lines and the caesura by a double line:

    ˘   ´   ˘   ´ ˘   ´ ˘   ´ ˘   ´
I knew | a wom|an, || love|ly in | her bones,

     ˘   ´   ˘   ´   ´ ˘   ˘   ´ ˘   ´
When small | birds sighed, || she would | sigh back | at them;

This indicates only roughly what the ear knows about the movement of these lines. All the accents are shown as equal, though of course they are not equal, and for that matter some of the unaccented syllables are weaker than others. Even the two caesuras are not the same. The limited choice of accent marks forces us to place an embarrassing weight on a preposition—the "in" of the first line—as if the line were being read in a grade-school, sing-song fashion. We're not comfortable putting it there, but we know that "in" accounts for one of the five stresses in the line.

The structural linguist recognizes four degrees of stress: *primary* (´), *secondary* (ˆ), *tertiary* (ˋ), and *weak* (˘). Using these to indicate the degree of accent on each of the syllables of the two lines, we have:

    ˋ   ˆ   ˘   ˆ ˋ   ´ ˘ ˋ ˘   ˆ
I knew a woman, | lovely in her bones,

     ˋ   ˆ   ˋ   ˆ   ´   ˋ   ˋ   ´ ˘   ˋ
When small birds sighed, | she would sigh back at them;

We can see some things now that we couldn't see before. For one, we understand that the assignment of a stress to "in" is correct, and it no longer seems awkward. While its accent is clearly not equal to that on "knew" or "bones," it is greater than the accents on adjacent syllables. This is what determines that a syllable's accent is counted as one of the stresses of a line. With the marks of conventional scansion, there was no way to show this. In the same way we understand the counting of the accent on "them" ending line 2 as a stress, because it is stronger than the only adjacent accent. For another thing, we see that the movement of the lines is not jerky, as the conventional marks, translated to an oscilloscope, would suggest:

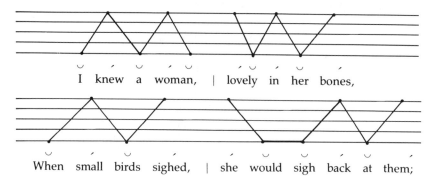

but is much more subtle:

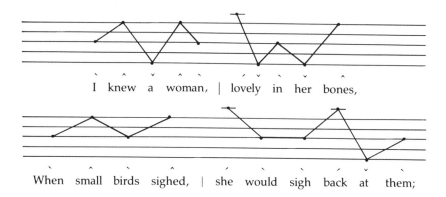

We can see the nuances more clearly now and in a way that might encourage young readers of poetry to drop the metronomic, foot-patting voice and read as if poetry were a human activity.

So much for stress; now the caesura. The structural linguist recognizes three types of breaks between words—*junctures*—that can serve us in the scanning of a poem. There is fading juncture (↓), rising juncture (↑) and sustained juncture (→). *Fading juncture* is what we have when the voice falls at the ends of most indicative sentences; *rising juncture* is what we have at the ends of most questions; *sustained juncture* occurs when a voice breaks into momentary silence without having risen or fallen perceptibly in pitch previous to the silence. For instance:

> →
> I know a place I'd like to take you to. ↓ Do you want to go? ↑

Obviously, fading juncture creates little if any expectation, sustained pitch creates a moderate degree, and rising juncture creates a great deal. The silences in a poem are an important part of what makes the poem work; they account in large measure for the tensions that give the poem much of its energy. We need to understand these silences if we're to understand the mechanics of poetry, the kind of silence, for instance, that Brooks and Warren call "the hovering effect"—as in the third line of Yeats's "After Long Silence": "Unfriendly lamplight hid under its shade." They use the term in *Understanding Poetry* (1950) to describe what happens between "light" and "hid"; the structural linguist describes it as sustained pitch: "light hid." The application of structural linguistics to this line is discussed by Ronald Sutherland in "Structural Linguistics and English Prosody" (*College English*, October, 1958).

Here are the two lines from Roethke's poem, marked for juncture:

> →
> I knew a woman, lovely in her bones, ↓
>
> When small birds sighed, ↑ she would sigh back at them; ↓

In this way we not only distinguish between the kinds of silences found in the lines, but we recognize that there are important silences at the ends of the lines. The type of juncture at the end of one line helps us to understand the beginning of the next line, since we tend to accent a syllable following rising juncture more than one following falling juncture. This is only a tendency, and not a rule, but it also helps to explain the stress on "she" in line 2, with the reversed foot.

For the prosodist who wants to show as much as can be shown

about the movement of a line, the structural linguist also recognizes gradations of pitch. These usually, but not always, vary directly with stress, since our voices generally get higher as we talk louder.

The range of low to high pitch is indicated by the numbers 1, 2, 3, and 4, in that order. If we now combine the indicators of stress, juncture, and pitch as they are applied to these lines—to my reading of these lines, anyway—we have this:

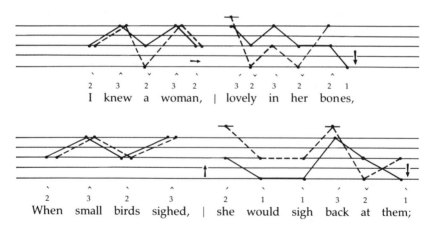

The movement of the lines then becomes as complex and subtle to the eye as it is to the ear, and we see what we get with each sound is— as Harold Whitehall has said—not so much a note as a chord. Putting it on an oscilloscope again, with a broken line for stress and a solid line for pitch, produces the following result.

Certainly no one would suggest this complex presentation as a substitute for conventional scansion, but for a closer study of a poem's movement, it makes possible a replicable vocal interpretation to a degree hardly approached by the use of standard prosodic signs. Perhaps it is worthwhile to remind ourselves now and then of how much of a poem's voice conventional scansion fails to take into account.

Appendix C: Some Observations on the Line

To pay attention to the line is not to suggest that a poem exists on the page. It doesn't. A poem comes into existence when the imagination of a writer and the imagination of a reader confront one another inside an act of language. The writer and the reader bring to that confrontation different imaginations structured by different associations. The poem in print is the ground on which the meeting takes place.

The line is the structural and functional unit of the printed poem, as decidedly as the paragraph is the unit of both structure and function in exposition and as the scene is in fiction. This is not to say that the line is necessarily a unit of sense, of course, but a poem doesn't work as a poem when the lines don't work as lines. The question is, what does it mean for a line to work? The answer is, to borrow a phrase of Auden's, simple and hard. It means that at the end of a line the reader feels rhythmically pleased but expectant. (In the case of the last line the expectation will be for nothing to follow, which is the most radical change in the poem.) It is this expectation that creates much of a good poem's sense of forward motion and—in the fulfillment of it—the sense of pleasure.

The anticipation created by the line's ending may be for the completion of a rhythmical pattern.

> Shave and a haircut
> Six bits

It may be for the completion of a statement, which is to say, simply, that the line is enjambed. In verse with a pattern of rhyme, the expectation is partly for the completion of the pattern each time a rhyme is begun. To speak of a pattern of rhyme is still to speak of the line, because rhyme (assuming that it's terminal) is a form of line break and thus is a function of the line.

Frequently, especially in freer verse—where there is no dependable pattern of rhyme and therefore no expectation—the end of a line will raise a question in the reader's mind, and the beginning of the next line will provide an answer. The following are some examples of how the reader is involved in this kind of juncture. From Louis Simpson's "American Poetry":

> Whatever it is, it must have
> A stomach that can digest
> Rubber, coal, uranium, moons, poems.

From Archibald MacLeish's "Winter Is Another Country":

> if this would end
> I could endure the absence in the night
> The hands beyond the reach of time, the name
> Called out.

This kind of juncture is also important in more formal verse, such as William Meredith's "The Open Sea":

> Nor does it signify, that people who stay
> Very long, bereaved or not, at the edge of the sea
> Hear the drowned folk call.

At the line breaks in these brief passages, a reader can ask—a good reader *will* ask—"What?" or "Then what?" or "How long?" The asking and the move to the answer not only propel the reader through the poem but heighten the reader's sense of participation in the poem.

Every time a word is added to a poem, the poet has made a decision about a line's relative and absolute length; every time a line is ended with a rhyme word, the poet makes a decision about the quality of sound setting up a rhyme set or decides whether to answer the first sound with true or slant rhyme. In the case of topographical or spatial poems like many of Cummings' and Ferlinghetti's, a decision is made about the placement of the line on the page. It is by all these means that a poet makes the line, and the poem, a more effective construction so that it becomes a more convincing illusion of conversation.

if a reader is to take part in the experience of a poem, the poem must be credibly of this world. We trust minds that talk our talk, and we are excited by minds that talk it with energy and leave as much as possible still to be said—minds, that is, that invite us into dialogue in our own language about the phenomenological world we live in. What is not always recognized is the intriguing relationship between reality and illusion.

Plain talk doesn't make for conversationality in poetry. The very fact of a poem is theatrical. We know that the realm of Prufrock is not the "real" world; it's an illusion of the world, or a part of it, as the stage is in a theater.

Reality in a framework of illusion (an actual living-room conversation in a play) or illusion in a context of reality (Lear's mad scene at a bus stop) gives a sense of the grotesque. Reality in a context of the "actual," phenomenological world or illusion in a context of a posited world gives a sense of the real.

This obviously invites a discussion of diction, but it is something that wants saying—I think it insists on being said—in an examination of any aspect of poetry, and it bears directly, as I mean to show, on the study of the line. The poet engineers the line and contrives line breaks so that the reader—in a context of illusion not unlike that represented by the proscenium arch—believes that the lines are natural things for a human to utter; the reader decides to believe it, that is, wants to and does, as we believe Hamlet when he is on the stage but not when he is on the sidewalk.

Poetry, like all art, is ritual, and ritual doesn't want conversation. The poet balances the two demands, plays conversationally against form, and finds in this tension much of the energy that means life to a poem.

Some of the most effective means of holding this balance, of heightening the sense of ritual or increasing the sense of spontaneity, are discovered in the way the lines end. *Enjambment* is the termination of a line at a point other than at the end of a phrase; it tends to increase the feeling of conversation. *End-stopping* is the cotermination of a line and a phrase or sentence; it tends to increase the feeling that the reader is involved in a ritual act.

Enjambment increases the sense of the lyric and compromises the ritualistic effect of rhyme. It was especially popular with the Elizabethan poets but—understandably—was not much favored by the neoclassicists. The romantic poets returned to the practice as an important aspect of their release from the formal strictures of the poetry of their recent past. The French, German, and Spanish histories have not been much different. Attitudes toward enjambment—from disapproval to tolerance to preference—have changed as the larger critical and aesthetic views of the society's literature have shifted.

Slant rhyme—as a form of line break—makes a poem more conversational than true rhyme, less conversational than no rhyme.

The metrics of the line break requires finer distinctions, but before turning to them, I feel compelled to make a statement correcting a general misapprehension about metrics: the nature of the foot at the end of a line is as relevant to nonpatterned poetry as it is to what we call formal poetry. No matter how purely accentual a line may be until the end, it is in the nature of the language that the last syllables in the line are going to be recognizable and that the reader is going to hear them as accented or not. This is the same thing as saying that the reader will recognize the terminal foot. The poet has to take this into account or lose some control over what the poem is doing.

An iambic or anapestic ending conveys a greater sense of formality than a trochaic or dactylic ending, or—to put it in less traditional terms—a final stress suggests greater seriousness than when the last stress is on the penultimate or an earlier syllable. The frequent use of the unstressed ending by the Elizabethan and Jacobean verse dramatists accounts for much of the apparent conversationality that marks their work.

Midway between these options is what is usually called the weak ending, an anapestic or iambic ending with less than full stress on the accent. This also tends to carry a suggestion of conversationality, but without risking the sense of lightness sometimes created by completely unaccented endings:

$$\smile \quad \acute{} \quad \smile \quad \acute{} \quad \smile \quad \acute{} \; \smile \; (\acute{})$$
I thought you sent the money in

This was a favorite device of Marianne Moore's; it is—with all her syllabics—a purely metrical consideration.

The omission of what would be a final unaccented syllable in a regular metrical line (called *truncation* or *catalexis*) is a useful device available to the poet writing in trochaic feet, because it helps to avoid the monotony that the trochaic line is likely to produce.

What am I supposed to say?

rather than:

What am I supposed to tell him?

Another option, obviously, is the length of the line itself. Most generalizations about this run into immediate contradictions. It is often said that as the line becomes shorter the poem becomes lighter, but then we have to take into account the fine small poem by Donald Justice, "Poem to Be Read at 3 A.M.," a moving and contemplative piece with one to three stresses per line, and most of Ogden Nash's comic poems, with lines like old fence rails.

What is probably safe to say about line length is that a line longer than six stresses is likely to be broken down in the reader's mind into smaller units, 5–2, 4–3, 5–3, or 4–4. It is also probably safe to say that the five-stress line is the most flexible line in English, the one to which most readers come and with fewest suspicions.

The last contact the poet has with the reader's imagination is in the poem's resolution; because of this, it's a highly important and sensitive moment in the poem's life. There are at least nineteen or twenty means by which a poet can change the reader's expectations so that the ending of a poem seems to be in the natural order of things; some of these function through the line break and changes in line length.

Here, as in all talk about poems, there are no hard rules. But there are principles that, when heeded, result most of the time in a more effective poem. This is all that rules can mean in poetry. I doubt if they mean more in any other art, but this makes the understanding of these principles and the use of them by the poet no less essential.

Three of the most important principles relating to closure as a function of the line are the following: A reader will tend to feel that it's right that the poem end 1) when a line is noticeably shorter or longer than the established line in the poem; 2) when an established pattern of terminal rhyme is modified or when a pattern is introduced where none had been; 3) when there is a shift from run-over to end-stopped lines. Examples of these types of closure can easily be found in most any anthology of poems from any period.

Much of the difference between verse and prose is found in the line and what it does. Prose "broken down" so that it has an uneven right margin does not become verse, because the length and ending of a line of verse are not arbitrary; they are contributing parts of an organism. And when a verse poem is put into paragraph form, something of what it does as a poem is lost.

The fact that good works sometimes lie uncertainly in more than one genre does not mean that the genres are not real. They are real, and the separate natures of the paragraph, the scene, and the line lie at the root of the distinctions between them. Our understanding of what a poem is starts with such an awareness.

Glossary of Additional Useful Terms

Note: For terms defined in the text, see Index.

ACATALECTIC. Describes a line of verse that is complete in its number of syllables. *See also* CATALECTIC.

CATALECTIC. Describes a line of verse in which the final unaccented syllable is omitted. *See also* ACATALECTIC.

CAUDATED. With added lines (on a stanza)

CURTAL. Shortened (said of a stanza or poem)

DIAERESIS. In classical prosody, denotes the slight break in the forward motion of a line that is felt when the end of a foot coincides with the end of a word. When this occurs after the fourth foot in dactylic verse, it is called *bucolic diaeresis*, because of its popularity among the writers of bucolic, or pastoral, poetry.

DIMETER. The measure of a line having two feet. Strictly, a double foot with a primary and a secondary stress and an unspecified number of unstressed syllables. The secondary stress may be represented by a pause.

DISTICH. A couplet

DOGGEREL. Any rhyming verse in which the meter is forced into metronomic regularity by the stressing of normally unstressed syllables and in which rhyme is forced or banal. Usually evokes humor, not always intentionally:

My love has grown from one small trickle
Since you rode by on your own tricycle.

EMBLEM. Originally a small woodcut or engraving, often of one or more animals, accompanied by a word (the *mot* or *motto*) conveying

189

the symbolic meaning of the picture and a brief verse (the *explication*) built on the idea in the picture. Often used now to denote only a verse written *as if* for such a purpose.

ENVELOPE. A verse unit in which a phrase or a line is repeated so as to enclose between its two occurrences other passages. An envelope may be a small part of a verse, a full stanza, or an entire poem of any length.

ENVOY. A (usually shortened) concluding stanza of a poem. Earlier it was the stanza of dedication, most often to a prince, by which a poem is sent on its way. From the French *envoyer*, to send.

EPIC. A long narrative told on a grand scale of time and place, featuring a larger-than-life protagonist and heroic actions

EPIGRAM. A brief, generally rhymed verse centering on a turn of wit

> What is an epigram? a dwarfish whole,
> Its body brevity, and wit its soul.
> > —Samuel Taylor Coleridge

> GOLD WATCH AT SIXTY

> Retired so early; what's living for?
> A flashlight burning in a drawer.
> > —William Cole

EPITAPH. Any EPIGRAM intended for a tombstone or written as if it were so intended. The latter sort, meant not to mark a grave but to stand on its own as a poem, is called a *literary epitaph*. Sometimes an epitaph intended for a grave can also be compelling as a poem, however, as seen in the first example below, copied from a stone in New Jersey. The second example is a *literary epitaph*.

> Reader pass on! Don't waste your time
> On bad biography and little rhyme;
> For what I am this crumbling clay insures
> And what I was is no affair of yours.

> Friend, on this scaffold Thomas More lies dead
> Who would not cut the Body from the Head.
> > —J. V. Cunningham

EYE RHYME. The relationship between words that look like rhymes but are not: *rough, though*

FABLIAU. A medieval French verse narrative, generally in eight-syllable lines, available in English most notably in the translations by John DuVal

FALSE RHYME. The relationship between words that would rhyme perfectly except that they have identical consonants immediately preceding the last accented vowel(s): *promotion, commotion.*

FEMININE RHYME. Rhyme involving both an accented and a following unaccented syllable: *rumble, tumble.* Also called *trochaic rhyme.*

FOOT. A metrical unit, as an iamb ($\cup$ /) or an anapest ($\cup\cup$ /). See Table of the Major Feet, p. 17.

FREE VERSE. Poetry in which line length and rhyme (if any) to come is not predictable from what has gone before nor prescribed by tradition.

GEORGICS. Instructions of any kind when written in verse

HALF RHYME. Assonance or consonance

HEAD RHYME. Rhyme set at the beginnings of lines

HEMISTICH. The half line on either side of a caesura

HENDECASYLLABICS. The measure of a line with eleven syllables; popular especially in formal Spanish poetry

HEPTAMETER. The measure of a line having seven feet

HEXAMETER. The measure of a line having six feet

HOMONYM. A word spelled and pronounced the same as another but different in meaning: *tip* (to cause something to lean) and *tip* (to leave money beyond the amount due for services)

HOMOPHONE. A word pronounced the same as another (whether spelled the same or not) but different in meaning: *blue, blew; sore, soar. See also* HOMONYM.

HUDIBRASTICS. Mock-heroic doggerel in iambic tetrameter, named after Samuel Butler's *Hudibras. See* MOCK.

HYPERMETER. The addition of unaccented syllables before or after an established line. See lines 1, 5, and 7 of Robert Bridges' "Triolet," p. 15.

IDYLL. A pastoral

INVERTED FOOT. The reversal of a foot so that stressed and unstressed syllables exchange places, as in the second foot of the following scansion:

$\cup$ / / $\cup$ $\cup$ / $\cup$ / $\cup$ /

MASCULINE RHYME. Rhyme involving only a terminal accented syllable: *ideal, conceal*

MOCK. Describes any satirical use of a serious form, as *mock epic, mock ode*

MONOMETER. The measure of a line having one foot

NEAR RHYME. Assonance or consonance

OCTAVE. An eight-line stanza

PAEAN. A poem of praise or celebration; originally a thanksgiving song to Apollo, after his Greek name *Paián*

PASTORAL. Any literary work about country life, especially when the people are dealt with in an idealized manner. Originally a poem or play about presumably pure, simple, and happy shepherds.

PENTAMETER. The measure of a line having five feet

PROSE POEM. A poem blocked as a prose paragraph, *i.e.*, without the poetic line as a unit

QUANTITATIVE METER. Meter created by alternating "long" and "short" syllables. A classical measure that has been tried in English with little success (*see also* QUANTITATIVE VERSE, p. 144).

RUN-ON LINE. An enjambed line

SCANSION. The examination of the meter of a unit of verse, or the visual representation of that meter

SLANT RHYME. Assonance or consonance

SPRUNG RHYTHM. The term used by Gerard Manley Hopkins to describe his relatively uneven, sometimes syncopated meter, created by the free use of extra unaccented syllables

STANZA. A group of lines constituting a formal division of a poem. The pattern of a stanza is usually repeated throughout the poem.

STAVE. A stanza beginning and ending with a refrain; a form of ENVELOPE:

I do not like thee, Dr. Fell.
Exactly why I cannot tell,
But this I know and know full well:
I do not like thee, Dr. Fell.

Originally STAVE denoted a stanza of a hymn or bawdy song or drinking song; many such songs were built on such a form, though usually with longer stanzas.

STICH. A line of verse

STROPHE. A movement in the PINDARIC ODE (see p. 126). Also, in modern poetry, a verse paragraph that, unlike the stanza, is not set by tradition or one of a repeated series.

SUBSTITUTION. The replacement of an established foot by another, as with the third foot in the following scansion:

‿/　‿/　‿‿/　‿/.　*See also* pp. 16 and 23.

TEXTURE. The effect created by the sensory suggestions of a poem's images, together with the actual physical experience of its sound and rhymes, as apart from its statement or idea

TONE. Mood, emotional quality, as in "tone of voice"

TRIMETER. The measure of a line having three feet

Selected Bibliography

Bayfield, Matthew Albert. *The Measures of the Poets*. Folcroft, Penn., 1970.

Beum, Robert, and Karl Jay Shapiro. *A Prosody Handbook*. New York, 1965.

Fussell, Paul. *Poetic Meter and Poetic Form*. New York, 1979.

Gross, Harvey Seymore. *The Structure of Verse*. Greenwich, Conn., 1966.

Gummere, Francis Barton. *A Handbook of Poetics for Students of English Verse*. Folcroft, Penn., 1973.

Lewis, Benjamin Roland. *Creative Poetry: A Study of Its Organic Principles*. Palo Alto, 1931.

Malof, Joseph. *A Manual of English Meters*. Westport, Conn., 1978.

Preminger, Alex, ed. *The Princeton Encyclopedia of Poetry and Poetics*. 2nd ed. Princeton, 1974.

Saintsbury, George. *History of English Prosody*. New York, 1966.

Smith, Barbara Herrnstein. *Poetic Closure*. Chicago, 1968.

Turco, Lewis. *The Book of Forms*. New York, 1968.

Wesling, Donald. *The Chances of Rhyme*. Berkeley, 1980.

Wimsatt, W. K. *Versification: The Major Language Types*. New York, 1972.

References to additional sources of information on prosody are available in the following volumes:

Brogan, T. V. F. *English Versification, 1570–1980: A Reference Guide with a Global Appendix*. Baltimore, 1981.

Shapiro, Karl Jay. *A Bibliography of Modern Prosody*. Baltimore, 1948.

Index of Authors, Titles, and Terms

Note: The patterns are in small capitals.